DATE DUE			

AN ATLAS OF
EUROPEAN AFFAIRS

AN ATLAS OF EUROPEAN AFFAIRS

text *by* Norman J. G. Pounds

maps *by* Robert C. Kingsbury

FREDERICK A. PRAEGER, *Publishers*
New York • Washington

BOOKS THAT MATTER

Published in the United States of America in 1964
by Frederick A. Praeger, Inc., Publishers
111 Fourth Avenue, New York 3, N.Y.

Library of Congress Catalog Card Number: MAP 64-4

Printed in The United States of America

Contents

71274

Foreword

Political crises multiply around the world, with political tension mounting in Laos or Pakistan, the Congo or Brazil. But always the spotlight returns to Europe. Despite the growing importance of Latin America and the non-Western world, Europe's importance in world politics does not appear to diminish. This is partly because Europe contains (after the North American continent) most of the principal centers of advanced industry, commercial agriculture, and modern technology in the modern world, and partly because the West and East here confront each other more directly than anywhere else. The two protagonists in the great conflict of the twentieth century are better placed in Europe than anywhere else to do battle for men's minds. Political affairs in all other parts of the world may increase and then diminish in their global significance, but those of Europe remain consistently and continuously important. The understanding of world politics is predicated on an appreciation of the European scene. This atlas attempts to portray that scene. The authors wish to thank Mrs. Susan S. Ball for her help in preparing the manuscript, and also Patricia R. Kingsbury for her assistance in completing the maps.

R. C. K.
N. J. G. P.

Bloomington, Indiana
September, 1963

1.   The Physical Map

Europe (excluding Soviet Russia) is the smallest of the continents. It covers little more than 3 per cent of the land surface of the globe, and is, in fact, merely an irregular peninsula thrust westward from the great land mass of Asia. It is flanked by the Arctic and Atlantic oceans, by the Mediterranean, Black, Caspian, and Aegean seas, and by the Ural and Caucasus Mountain ranges. Lesser peninsulas extend from it, enclosing long branches of the sea, some of which— such as the Baltic, Adriatic, and White seas—penetrate deeply into the continent. Europe is characterized by the length and complexity of its coastline, by its many peninsulas, and by the fringe of islands that encloses it. Of the hundreds of islands around the coast of Europe, most are small, and many are uninhabited. Iceland and Spitsbergen (Svalbard) are large, but they lie too far to the north to be populous or economically as important as the major European nations. By far the most significant of the island groups is the British Isles, lying off the continent's northwest coast. Other important island groups are those of Denmark, the Baltic, and many in the Mediterranean Sea (particularly Corsica, Sardinia, Sicily, and Crete).

Europe is a varied continent. Stretching across it from west to east is a chain of high mountains that includes the Pyrenees, the Alps, and the Carpathian mountains and their extensions in the Balkan Peninsula. Despite the many gaps that open routes across these mountains, they do form a kind of division between north and south. Between the Alpine mountains and the Mediterranean Sea are the southern peninsulas of Europe, made up of hills, plateaus, and small coastal plains. There are also such north-south mountain chains as the Apennines, Dinaric Mountains, and Rhodope Mountains. To the north of the mountains lies a belt of hills made up of old, hard rock; the soil is poor, and the area is, for the most part, thinly populated and forested. These hills sink into the Great Plain of Northern Europe. This region of level plain and low, rounded hills begins in France and broadens eastward until it merges into the plains of Russia. Much of it was glaciated during the Ice Age and is today covered with glacial deposits. This part of the European Plain is still strewn with sandy moraines, left by the ice sheets, and dotted with small lakes. Farther to the north, in Finland, Scandinavia, and the northern and western parts of the British Isles, the land is

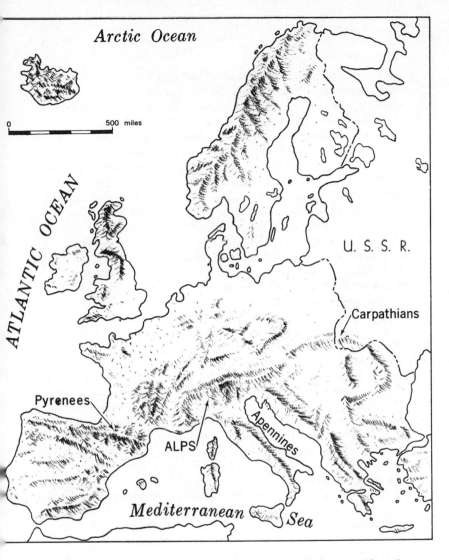

built of older and harder rocks and is more mountainous, although
the mountains themselves are more rounded and worn down than the
sharp and rugged Alps. In Norway, Sweden, and Finland, this region
is known as the Scandinavian Shield.

3

2. Climate

Europe lies between the latitudes of 36° and 71° N. Much of it lies in the same latitude as Canada, yet the climate of most of the continent is quite different from Canada's. The dominant influence on the climate throughout the continent is its proximity to the sea. No point is more than 500 miles from salt water. The prevailing winds over most of the continent are from the west, and they carry influences of the Atlantic Ocean far inland. The temperature of the ocean itself is moderated by the drift of relatively warm water—the North Atlantic Drift—which is driven from the Gulf of Mexico northeastward across the ocean to the shores of Europe. In the coastal areas, the warmth of the sea is carried inland by the winds in winter, and the sea breezes have a cooling influence on the land in summer.

Europe can be divided into two climatic regions, separated from each other roughly by the line of the Alps and related mountains. North of this line, Europe lies most of the time in the path of cyclonic disturbances that move in from the Atlantic. Winds are predominantly from the west. Rainfall is generous in all seasons—heaviest in the mountains and diminishing as one moves eastward toward the Soviet Union. Temperatures range from the mild and almost frost-free winters of western France and the west coast of the British Isles to relatively severe winters in Central and Eastern Europe. Summer temperatures are cool near the Atlantic and correspondingly warmer the farther inland one goes. The over-all range of temperature increases from west to east. The climate of the coastal regions is described as "maritime," that of the interior as "continental." The severity of the climate increases as one goes northward. In Scandinavia and Finland, winters are long, cold, and very snowy; summers are short and cool.

South of the Alps, the climate is generally influenced by the Mediterranean. This area does not usually receive the moist west winds in summer, since the storm tracks have moved north during this season. Summers are generally hot and dry. The Mediterranean area has cyclonic storms in winter, and most of its rainfall occurs then. The vegetation of the Mediterranean region is closely adapted to its temperature and rainfall (*see Map 3*).

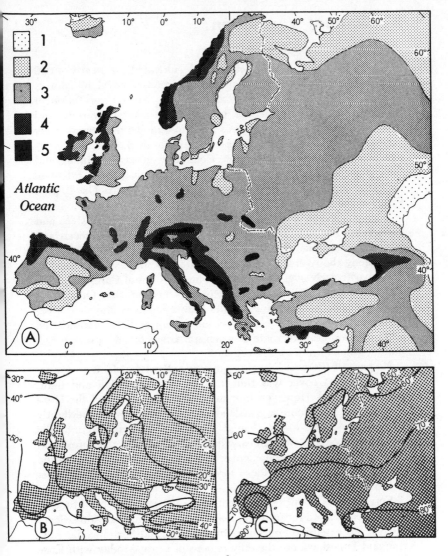

A. *Average annual precipitation in inches:*
   1—under 10; *2*—10 to 20; *3*—20 to 30; *4*—40 to 60; *5*—60 or more. Degrees of latitude and longitude indicated at edge of map
B. *Average January temperature in degrees F.* (reduced to sea level)
C. *Average July temperature in degrees F.* (reduced to sea level)

3. Natural Vegetation

A continent that has been settled and cultivated for nearly 4,000 years will not have much of its natural vegetation cover remaining. Originally, Europe was a forested land. The natural vegetation of the Mediterranean region was of a drought-resistant variety and was deep-rooted, with thin leaves like those of the mimosa or waxy leaves like those of the camellia—resulting from the long, hot, dry summers and mild, rainy winters. Conifers were also common, and throughout large areas there was—and still is, to a great extent—a thicket of low-growing bushes, often known as *maquis*. The Iberian Peninsula has extensive areas of dry grassland.

The rain comes in all seasons in the Alpine mountain system and north of it. The natural vegetation cover was forest: the beech and ash in the limy soils; elm, oak, and hazel in the clay; and willow and alder along the rivers. Where the climate was more severe, conifers grew, particularly over the higher ground in Central Europe and the plains of Eastern Europe. They were also the dominant forest trees of Scandinavia and Finland. In the high mountains and in the extreme north, where the climate is too severe and the summer too short for tree growth, there is a natural cover of low-growing "alpines," which form a tundra vegetation.

No parts of Western Europe were ever natural grassland or steppe, although forest cover was thin in areas of low rainfall and light, well-drained soil. However, human use has caused part of the Hungarian Plain to become a grassland. Settlement began in the lightly wooded and more easily cleared areas, and later spread into the more densely forested regions. The task of clearing the forest and creating settlements was done over much of the continent during the Middle Ages, but the northern forests have only begun to be penetrated in recent years.

Forest covers about 30 per cent of the area of Europe. Much of it has been planted recently in areas of little agricultural value. Scandinavia has extensive areas of natural forest, and Scandinavia, Austria, and Yugoslavia are the only regions of Europe today with large timber surpluses. In fact, lumber products constitute most of the exports of Finland. Several countries have planted quick-growing conifers over areas of infertile soil that is unfit for modern agriculture. Such re-afforestation is important on the sandy *landes* of France, on the heaths of Belgium, the Netherlands, and Germany, and on the moors of Great Britain.

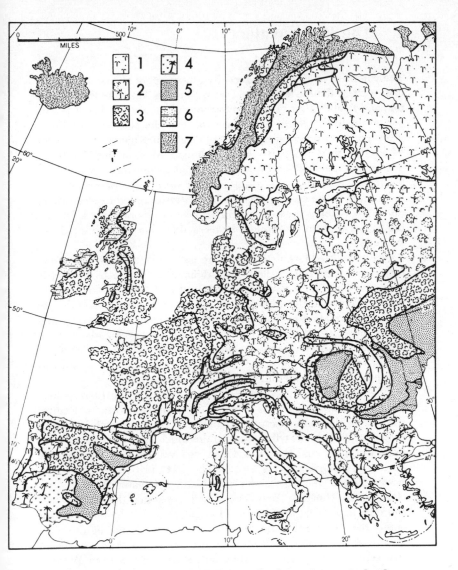

1—coniferous forest; *2*—mixed coniferous-deciduous forest; *3*—deciduous forest (semideciduous in Spain); *4*—Mediterranean vegetation; *5*—grass; *6*—heath and moor; *7*—alpine and tundra

4. The Waterways

The continent of Europe is laced by a network of rivers. The larger ones west of the Soviet border rise within the Alpine mountain system and flow either to the Mediterranean basin or the Black Sea or northward to the North or Baltic seas. The characteristics of European rivers are determined partly by the nature of the terrain over which they flow and partly by the climate. Most of the Mediterranean rivers are short and torrent-like, and many drop steeply from the mountains to the sea. Many run dry during the period of summer drought. The northern rivers, by contrast, are fed by year-round rains. Their flow is greatest in winter, when evaporation is least, but the largest of them continue to be navigable even through the driest summers.

Not many Mediterranean rivers are navigable, and the sharp fluctuations in their rate of flow pose difficulties for the hydroelectric engineer. The Rhone rises in Switzerland and flows through southeastern France to the Mediterranean Sea; it has been canalized to improve navigation in its lower course. The chief rivers of the Iberian Peninsula—the Tagus, Douro, and Ebro—vary greatly in their flow and are not navigable except in their lowermost courses. Only the River Po, in northern Italy, has a strong summer flow, and this is due largely to the melting snows of the Alps.

The most important North European rivers are the Loire, which is not really navigable; the Seine, in western and northern France; the Rhine, the most easily navigated and most used of European rivers, which, with its tributaries, drains much of eastern France and West Germany; and the Elbe, Oder, and Vistula. The Danube, the longest of European rivers, rises to the north of the Alpine system, passes through the Alps and Carpathians in Bavaria, Austria, Czechoslovakia, Hungary, and Yugoslavia, separates the Carpathians from the Balkans on the borders of Romania and Bulgaria, and then enters the Black Sea. The Danube is potentially one of the most important rivers in Europe, but its usefulness has been greatly restricted by postwar political divisions, since it flows from Western to Communist Europe and there is no great volume of trade between Western and Eastern Europe. The Danube, however, is used to a considerable extent in the trade between the Soviet Union and some of its East European satellites. The North European rivers have been linked by a series of canals across the Great Plain, which is

8

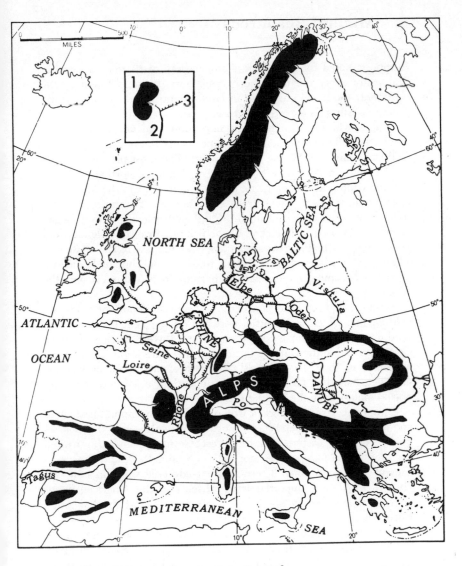

1—main mountain area; *2*—major river; *3*—canal

well adapted to their construction and maintenance. Theoretically, it is possible to navigate a small river barge from the west coast of France to Moscow or Bulgaria.

9

5.   Mineral Resources

Europe is noted for the richness and variety of its mineral wealth. Practically every mineral of economic importance is found in the continent, and many are found in large quantities, thus contributing greatly to Europe's industrial stature.

Coal is widespread. The most important coal fields are located where the hilly belt of Central Europe meets the northern plain, as well as in England, Wales, and Scotland. The most productive ones are in southern Poland, West Germany, Belgium, northern France, and the United Kingdom. Little coal is obtained from the Mediterranean countries, and none from Scandinavia. European industry relies heavily on coal, and until oil and hydroelectric power began to be widely used in industry, Great Britain, France, Belgium, and West Germany had a great advantage over the rest of the continent. There is still a large and important trade in coal, but hydroelectric power is becoming increasingly important in Scandinavia and the Alpine regions.

Europe produces little petroleum. The most important fields are in Romania, which yields little more than 1 per cent of the world's production. Petroleum is also found in southwest France, in West Germany, and in the Danube basin; and there are important natural-gas fields in Italy, France, and the Netherlands. Most of Europe, however, including Great Britain, is dependent upon petroleum imported mainly from the Middle East.

Europe has large reserves of iron ore. The most important of these are the high-grade deposits of northern Sweden and the poorer-quality ores of eastern France, West Germany, and the United Kingdom. There are smaller deposits in Spain, Italy, and the countries of Eastern Europe. There is a considerable trade in iron ore. High-quality ore is imported from Africa and the American continent, as it is generally not worth while to transport the low-grade European ores more than a short distance.

Deposits of nonferrous metals are widespread, but these are no longer as important as they once were. The copper deposits of Spain and Sweden, the lead and zinc of Spain and Poland, and the tin of Cornwall are still mined, but for many years these have constituted a diminishing proportion of the total world output. Italy, Spain, and Yugoslavia still produce a major part of the world's mercury, but non-European production increased as a result of World War II.

10

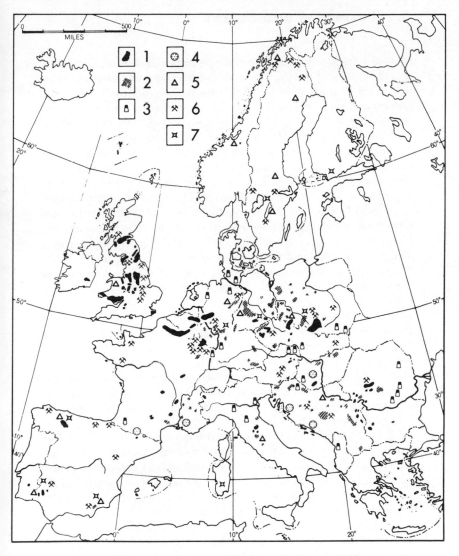

Major mineral deposits: 1—coal; 2—lignite; 3—petroleum; 4—bauxite; 5—copper; 6—iron ore; 7—lead and zinc

Bauxite, the ore from which aluminum is obtained, is found in large quantities in southern France, Hungary, and Yugoslavia.

6. Farmland and Forest

Most of Europe is suited to agriculture, although climatic conditions and the quality of the soil vary greatly from one area to another. The only areas that are quite unsuitable for farming are the high mountain regions and some parts of northern Scandinavia (because of the severe climate). Within the rest of the continent, there is a sharp contrast between the Mediterranean basin and Northern Europe. Winter and spring are the growing seasons in the Mediterranean basin, and crops ripen during the hot and very dry summer months. Tree crops, such as olives, and vine crops, such as grapes, are most important in Mediterranean agriculture. There is a scarcity of fodder crops, which wither in the dry summer; as a result dairy cattle are few. While their cattle have increased in number in recent years, the Mediterranean countries still depend for dairy products on sheep and goats. The grazing habits of these animals have played an important part in the destruction of forests in the area. Irrigation is important in some restricted areas, especially in southern Spain and parts of Italy.

North of the Alps, the growing season lasts through the summer, but in the north and east, severe winters stop the growth of plants and greatly restrict the range of crops that can be grown. The northwestern margin of the continent is characterized by cool summers, mild winters, and an abundance of rainfall—factors that encourage the growth of grass and fodder crops. Thus, dairy farming is especially important in northwest France, the British Isles, the Low Countries, and Scandinavia.

To the east, the climate is drier and the winters colder. Grass and fodder crops are less important, and farming consists mainly in growing cereals, potatoes, and sugar beets. Local conditions of climate and soil determine the actual combination of crops, but in general rye is grown in the poorer soil and wheat in the better. Oats for fodder and barley for brewing are also grown. The soil in Northern Europe is poorer and the growing season shorter than in Central and Southern Europe. Grass, fodder crops, and (locally) flax are more important than wheat, and the forested area is larger.

The cultivation of vegetables and produce is important near the cities, and in some particularly favored areas, such as the south and west of France and the mild southwest of the British Isles, early vegetables, potatoes, and flowers are grown for distant urban markets.

12

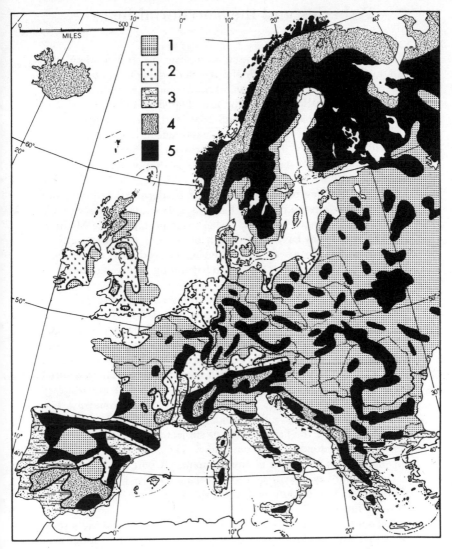

1—cropland; *2*—cropland and pasture; *3*—Mediterranean agriculture; *4*—wasteland and some pasture; *5*—forest

7. Fisheries and the Territorial Sea

Europe is surrounded by an area of shallow sea (up to about 600 feet in depth) beyond which the sea floor deepens quite sharply. This shallow sea is the Continental Shelf, and it is particularly important as a breeding ground for fish. The shelf underlies most of the North Sea, encloses the British Isles, and is very conspicuously developed along the coast of Scandinavia and around Iceland—the chief fishing grounds. The seas off northwest Europe are especially rich in fish, and the fisheries constitute an important part of the national economy in Iceland, Norway, and the United Kingdom. There are fisheries in all the countries bordering the ocean, but these are not important in the Baltic Sea, because of the variable salinity of the water. While tuna-fishing is important in the Mediterranean, other types have lagged both because of the comparatively small quantities of such species as herring and cod to be found there and because of the lack of modern refrigerating facilities in much of the area.

All European states that have a coastline claim sovereignty over some part of the adjacent sea. The traditional 3-mile limit, based on the range of eighteenth-century cannon, is no longer widely accepted, although Great Britain still adheres to it for most purposes. Other countries assert jurisdiction over varying distances, ranging up to 12 miles for all purposes and much more for some. The territorial sea is usually measured from the low-tide mark, but an arbitrary base line farther out to sea has been taken by some countries. For example, both Norway and Iceland, for the openly expressed purpose of increasing the fishing grounds subject to their own sovereign control, have extended their base lines. The Norwegian claim was the subject of a judgment of the Permanent Court of International Justice in Norway's favor in 1951. Iceland's claim was the subject of an acrimonious dispute with the United Kingdom, now settled in Iceland's favor.

A claim to sovereignty over the territorial waters bordering a state gives that state exclusive control not only over its fisheries but also over minerals that may lie beneath the sea bed. It also allows the state to exclude ships and aircraft from the area. This is perhaps the most important reason why the Communist countries claim a much wider area.

14

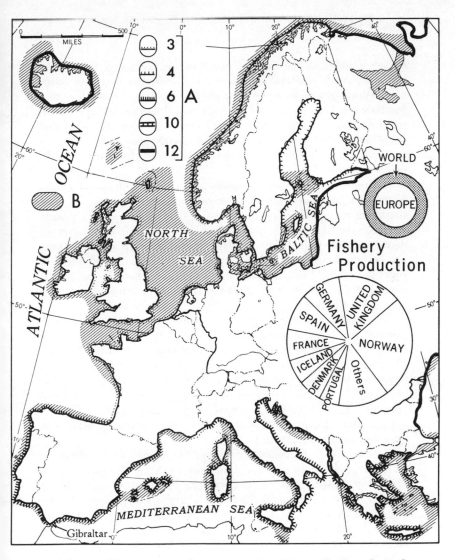

A. *Claims over territorial waters: 3, 4, 6, 10,* and *12*—miles from low-tide mark (coastline) or arbitrary base line, as indicated

B. *Major fishing grounds*

Concentric circles show Europe's proportion of total world fishery production; circle graph shows relative proportion of individual states in total European fishery production

15

8. Population

Europe (excluding the Soviet Union) has an estimated total population of about 430 million, unevenly distributed over the continent. Population tends to be most dense in a west-to-east belt that lies between Scandinavia on one side and the Alps and the Mediterranean basin on the other (although such densely populated countries as Italy and Switzerland fall outside this area), and it is relatively sparse in parts of Scandinavia and the Alps and the Mediterranean basin.

The region of very dense population begins in the west in the United Kingdom and stretches across northern France, the Low Countries, central Germany, southern Poland and neighboring parts of Czechoslovakia, and into the Ukraine. This area has an over-all density of more than 225 persons per square mile. In addition, there is a belt reaching up the Rhine Valley to Switzerland, and much of Italy, the Rhone Valley of southeastern France, and the peripheral regions of the Iberian Peninsula have population densities considerably above the average.

This higher density corresponds in some degree to the region of superior soil and prosperous agriculture, but it can probably be attributed more directly to the presence of manufacturing industries, which employ the majority of the population, and the ancillary services these industries require. There is also a close relationship between this belt of dense population and the location of coal deposits (*see Map 5*). (There are, of course, many other significant factors in population density—historical, cultural, the location of other raw materials and resources, etc.)

In other areas, the density of population tends to vary generally with the productivity of the soil and the facility of communication. It is fairly dense in northern and western France, over much of the North European Plain, and down the Danube Valley. North of the latitude of about 60° N., the severity of the climate restricts agriculture and makes industrial activity (except mining) almost impossible. Most of Scandinavia is very thinly populated.

Within the Mediterranean basin, the rugged terrain and prolonged summer drought greatly restrict agriculture. The industrial population, except in Italy, is small, and the rural and agricultural population is sparse.

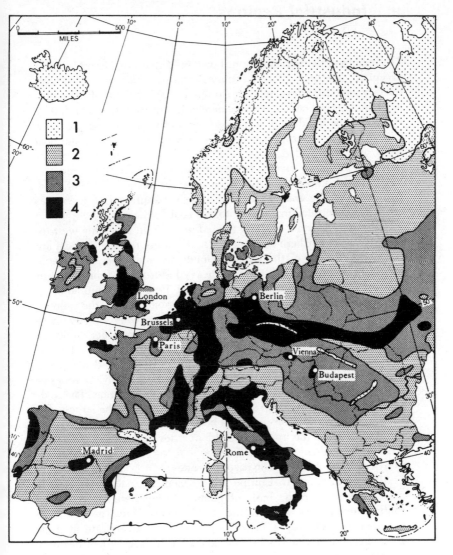

Number of people per square mile:
1—under 25; *2*—25 to 125; *3*—125 to 250; *4*—250 or more

9. Industrial Regions

The regions of dense population shown in Map 8 are, almost without exception, engaged more in manufacturing than in agriculture. Factory industries developed in Europe toward the end of the eighteenth and in the first half of the nineteenth centuries. In general, they antedated the building of a railroad net and were attracted to areas with good water transport, natural resources such as wool, and coal fields, which provided much of their fuel, or to sources of water power. With improvements in transportation and the use of alternative forms of power, there has been some dispersion of manufacturing; however, the greater part of Europe's manufacturing industries are still concentrated in, or close to, the coal-field areas.

The most important of these (*see Map 5*) lie in a roughly west-to-east belt, from northern England to the Ukraine. In or near them are concentrated most of the United Kingdom's iron, steel, and textile industries, a large part of France's heavy industry, and almost all of the textile and metallurgical industries of Belgium. Manufacturing industries developed somewhat later in Germany—after the railroad system had been built. German factories were thus initially more widespread than in many other countries, because fuel could be more easily transported. Nevertheless, a striking concentration of industry developed in and near the Ruhr coal field and along the Rhine River. Manufacturing industries in East Germany, Czechoslovakia, and Poland are also located in or near coal-field areas. The coalfields of the Ruhr (*see Map 31*) and of Upper Silesia—the largest and most productive in Europe—have become the sites of the heaviest concentrations of the iron and steel industries. Other important centers are the coal-field areas of Belgium and Northern France and the iron-ore region of Lorraine in eastern France.

Alpine and Southern Europe are deficient in coal. Hydroelectric power has become the basis of manufacturing here, especially in southeastern France, Switzerland, and northern Italy (as well as in Scandinavia). Factory industries developed relatively late in these areas, because power has become available in large quantities only in recent years. There is a sharp contrast between the clean and smokeless industrial cities of Scandinavia and the Alpine regions, and the dirty, congested, and poorly planned industrial regions that grew up in the coal-field regions during the nineteenth century. Throughout Europe, petroleum has been outstripping coal as a

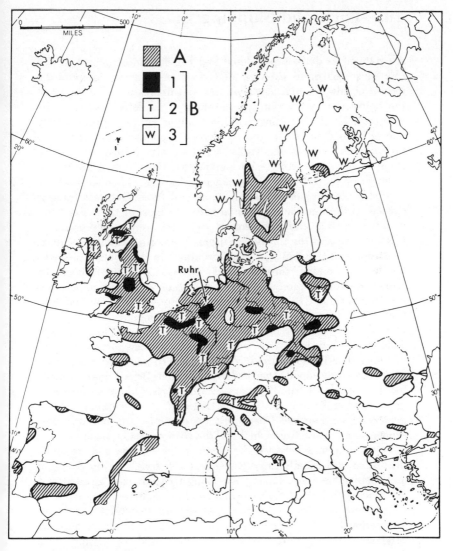

A. *Major industrial region*
B. *Industrial Concentrations: 1*—metallurgical; *2*—textile; *3*—woodworking

source of power, and countries such as France and Italy, with large reserves of natural gas, have been relying increasingly on it.

10. Ports and Shipping

A continent as densely populated and heavily industrialized as Europe must necessarily carry on a large volume of trade. Many of the industrial raw materials, such as ores and fibers, as well as most of the petroleum and varying proportions of foodstuffs, have to be imported. The United Kingdom, for example, imports approximately half of its food supply. In return, European countries export factory products and certain foodstuffs, and they also furnish services in transportation, commerce, and banking to other parts of the world.

Much of the trade of European countries is with one another—carried on by way of rail, road, canal, and river. Overseas trade is carried on through the continental seaports; most of the bulky commodities—such as grain, ore, cotton, wool, and lumber—are imported this way. Around the shores of Europe, there are a number of ports of exceptional size and importance. Largest in the volume of goods handled is London, through which passes about one-fifth of the United Kingdom's foreign commerce. Also of very great importance are Hamburg and Bremen in West Germany; Amsterdam and Rotterdam in the Netherlands; Antwerp in Belgium; Dunkirk, Le Havre, and Marseilles in France; Genoa and Naples in Italy; and Göteborg in Sweden. There are also many smaller ports, a number of which handle specialized commodities. In recent years several ports have developed (particularly in Great Britain and France) for the purpose of handling petroleum imports. Others specialize in grain, lumber, or iron ore, in exporting coal, or in handling passengers. Southampton and Cherbourg, for example, are primarily passenger ports, to and from which sail the chief transatlantic liners.

Regular sailings between the continent of Europe and its many peninsulas and islands carry passengers and freight. Most frequent and regular are those linking the Danish islands and Sweden and those between Ireland, Great Britain, and the continent.

The few countries with no coastline are dependent for their international trade on the use of ports of other countries and the privilege of transporting goods across their neighbors' territory. In a few instances, an inland state has a free zone in the port of a neighbor —for example, as Yugoslavia has in Salonika (*see Map 43*).

All the larger ports and many of the smaller ones have developed industries particularly associated with seaborne trade. These include shipbuilding and the preparation of imported food and raw materials.

20

1—major port; 2—major internal sea service; 3—major waterway; 4—country with no direct access to the sea

11. Language Groups

The approximately 430 million Europeans speak, among them, no fewer than 30 languages, in addition to numerous dialects. These distinctive language groups have constituted the most important factor influencing the course of political boundaries. Some language groups, such as most of the Celtic tongues and some of the Romance languages spoken in the Alps, are declining in importance and no longer form the dominant languages of any state. Others, such as Catalan in Spain and Macedonian in Yugoslavia, have only recently developed into literary languages from what had previously been dialects.

Most European languages belong to one of four separate language groups:

1) The Romance languages derive from Latin, which was spread over the Mediterranean basin and beyond by the armies of the Roman Empire. The chief languages of this group are Italian, Spanish, Portuguese, French, and Romanian (which has, however, absorbed a good deal of Slavic). In addition, the Romance languages include Romansch and other obscure tongues still spoken in the Alps.

2) The Germanic languages originated in the Baltic region and were carried southward into Central Europe by the Germanic invaders, westward to Great Britain by the Anglo-Saxons, northward through Norway and Sweden across the ocean to Iceland, and west of the Rhine (which had been the boundary of the Roman Empire) by invaders. Today German is spoken in eastern France, and the Germanic language Flemish is spoken in northern Belgium. The western boundary of Germanic speech has hardly been altered for centuries, but its eastern boundary has been changed by the population shifts that accompanied and followed World War II.

3) The Slavic languages have spread from the general area of modern Poland southward into the Danube basin and the Balkans, and eastward into Russia.

4) The Uralic group of languages, deriving from Central Asia and brought into Europe by invaders, is represented by Hungarian, Finnish, and Estonian, and by the languages of the Lapps and other seminomadic peoples of the Arctic.

In addition to these languages, which developed and spread during historical times, there are languages that were spoken here before the beginnings of written history. These include Albanian and Basque.

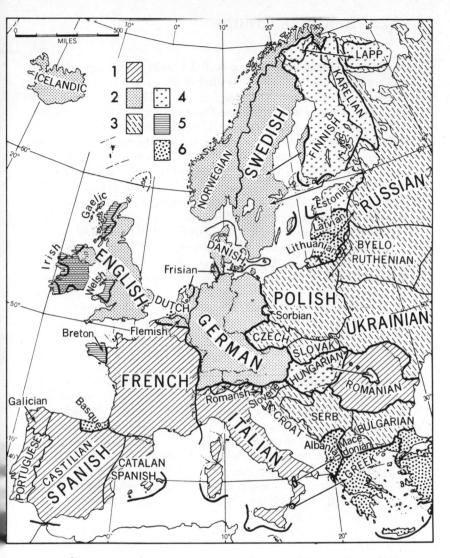

Major language families: 1—Romance; 2—Germanic (Teutonic); 3—Slavic; 4—Uralic; 5—Celtic; 6—others

12.   Religious Groups

Religion, like language, is an aspect of human culture, and the distribution of religious faiths, like that of languages, is an important factor in political organization and relations. The relation of church and state varies widely from one European country to another. Although only about half have established churches, state subsidies of one sort or another to one or more churches are common in several others—including some Communist-bloc countries—and churches often play a role in education. The division of Europe into several different religious faiths is important in shaping the attitudes of the people and in adding to the intensity of local and patriotic feeling.

Most Europeans accept one of the branches of the Christian faith. These divisions correspond, to a degree, with the linguistic groupings. Among the Romance-speaking peoples of Italy, France, Belgium, and the Iberian Peninsula, most church members are Roman Catholic. Catholicism is also strong in Ireland, Austria, Hungary, northern Yugoslavia, most of Czechoslovakia, all of Poland, southern Germany, Lithuania, the southern Netherlands, and parts of Switzerland. Protestantism, which originated in northern Germany, is dominant in the Scandinavian lands and Finland, the Netherlands, the United Kingdom, Latvia, Estonia, and parts of Hungary, Romania, and Czechoslovakia. The Orthodox, or Eastern churches, which separated gradually from the Roman Catholicism of the West during the earlier Middle Ages, prevail in the Balkan Peninsula. Clashes between these groups—as, for example, between the Catholic Croats and the Orthodox Serbs in Yugoslavia—have sometimes had strong political overtones. In some countries, such as Ireland, Poland, and Spain, allegiance to the church has at times been so strong as to be virtually an expression of national feeling. The Jewish population of Eastern and Central Europe is only a fraction of what it was before World War II, although there are still more than 2 million Jews in the Soviet Union and about a half-million in other East European countries, chiefly Romania and Hungary. In some West European countries, however, they are more numerous than before the war. This is particularly true in France, where the number has been increased by immigrants both from Eastern Europe and from North Africa, and to a lesser extent in England, which has also given a home to many refugees. There are significant numbers of Moslems in European Turkey, Albania, Yugoslavia (where they form a majority of the Bosnian population), Greece (where they are a majority in

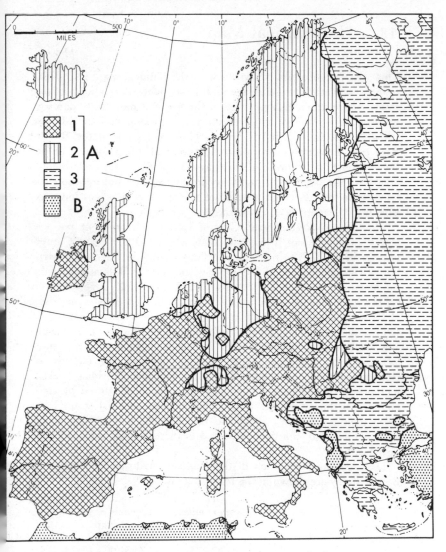

A. *Christian:* 1—Roman Catholic; 2—Protestant; 3—Orthodox
B. *Moslem*

some districts of Thrace), Bulgaria, and Cyprus; there are also hundreds of thousands of North African Moslems living in France.

13. The Political Map

This atlas is concerned primarily with the political map, for all European problems are conditioned by the political relations among states. There are in Europe west of the Soviet Union thirty-one sovereign states—plus two small territories (Gibraltar and the Maltese Islands) that are colonial in status. These thirty-one states, for the most part, reflect the aspirations for political independence of nations distinct in culture and language. In some cases, their boundaries have the sanction of many generations of use, but in others the boundaries are new, and several of the states themselves have existed for little more than a generation.

Throughout Western and Central Europe, the present political map is little different from that created by the Paris Peace Conference in 1919–20. The most conspicuous change has been the partition of Germany. Even in Eastern Europe and the Balkan Peninsula, the boundary changes that have occurred since 1945 have not been far-reaching, except in the westward shift of Poland. A comparison of the map drawn after World War I with the one that existed at the beginning of the century shows a much more profound change. The maps of Central and Eastern Europe are not even broadly similar. The area was then mostly divided between the empires of Germany, Russia, and Austria-Hungary, with a diminishing Turkish foothold in the Balkans. These empires were all shattered by military defeat during World War I, and smaller national states have taken their place. Only along the Iron Curtain between the Communist bloc and the free world are there significant territorial disputes.

The area and population of the political territories that make up Europe today are shown in the following table:

	Area (in square miles)	Population	Persons per square mile
Albania	11,099	1,660,000	149
Andorra	175	9,000	51
Austria	32,374	7,081,000	218
Belgium	11,779	9,184,000	779
Bulgaria	42,829	7,943,000	185
Czechoslovakia	49,370	13,776,000	227
Denmark	17,159	4,617,000	269
Finland	130,119	4,467,000	34
France	212,821	45,960,000	215
Germany, East (includes East Berlin)	41,635	17,125,000	413

Germany, West (includes West Berlin)	95,920	56,225,000	583
Gibraltar	2.3	27,000	11,739
Greece	50,547	8,402,000	166
Hungary	35,919	10,028,000	279
Iceland	39,768	179,000	5
Ireland (Eire)	27,136	2,815,000	104
Italy	116,300	49,455,000	433
Liechtenstein	61	17,000	273
Luxembourg	999	317,000	317
Malta	122	329,000	2,695
Monaco	0.6	22,000	38,576
Netherlands	12,616	11,637,000	923
Norway	149,165	3,611,000	24
Poland	120,359	29,965,000	249
Portugal	35,527	9,196,000	257
Romania	91,699	18,567,000	202
San Marino	24	17,000	696
Soviet Union (European)	1,850,000	168,000,000	90
Spain	194,880	30,559,000	156
Sweden	173,649	7,520,000	43
Switzerland	15,941	5,496,000	343
Turkey (European)	9,200	2,300,000	250
United Kingdom	93,895	53,082,000	563
Vatican City	0.2	1,000	5,882
Yugoslavia	98,766	18,607,000	187

14.   The British Isles

The British Isles constitute the largest group of islands off the European coast. They consist of two main islands—Great Britain (comprising England, Scotland, and Wales) and Ireland—a number of smaller inhabited islands, and numerous small islets and rocks that are of no economic value and even constitute a danger to shipping. At its nearest point, Great Britain lies 20 miles from the coast of continental Europe. No narrow sea has ever been more significant than this one, for it has given Great Britain a degree of immunity to invasion and conquest unknown in continental Europe. This has permitted an almost uninterrupted development of political institutions and civil liberties. The British Isles have, however, been invaded from the continent on several occasions, and the lowland plain of southeastern Britain has been overrun and subjugated, but no foreign invasion has been successful since the Norman Conquest of 1066. Ancient peoples and cultures have tended to survive in mountainous and rugged Wales and northern Scotland and in Ireland, where the Celtic language (*see Map 11*) has been preserved and is a factor in the strong nationalism of Ireland and the less intense local feeling of Wales.

The British Isles are divided politically into (a) the United Kingdom of Great Britain and Northern Ireland and (b) the Republic of Eire. The United Kingdom is made up of England (with fourfifths of the population), Wales, Scotland, and Northern Ireland. Wales is integrated with England in law and administration, but unlike England has no established church. Scotland is separate from England in certain aspects of its legal and administrative systems, and the Presbyterian rather than the Episcopal Church is the established Church of Scotland. Northern Ireland has a form of home rule, with a separate parliament and Prime Minister, although it is represented in the British Parliament and has contributed many members to British cabinets. Not all legislation passed by the Parliament in London automatically applies to either Scotland or Northern Ireland. In addition, the Isle of Man and the French-speaking Channel Islands are considered dependencies, rather than parts, of the United Kingdom; they have their own parliaments, judicial institutions, and bodies of law, as well as local administrations, and acts of Parliament do not apply to them unless specifically so stated. The national government in London contains Ministers of State for Welsh and Scottish Affairs.

The government of Great Britain retains some political control over the dependent Empire, but not over the self-governing members of the Commonwealth, with which the United Kingdom is joined by ties of sympathy and mutual self-interest.

The United Kingdom now has two major political parties, the Conservative Party and the Labour Party; the Liberal Party has been very small in recent years. The Prime Minister is nominally selected by the monarch, but is usually the leader of whichever party has a majority in the elected House of Commons. The Labour Party, under Clement Attlee, came to power in 1945, but was replaced in 1951 by the Conservatives, under the leadership of Winston Churchill. In 1955, Churchill resigned and was succeeded both as leader of the party and as Prime Minister by Sir Anthony Eden, who was in turn followed by Harold Macmillan in 1957. Macmillan resigned for reasons of health in October, 1963, and Sir Alec Douglas-Home was appointed as his successor. A new election will be held in 1964, and the next Prime Minister may well be the Labour leader, Harold Wilson.

29

15. The United Kingdom—Resources and Planning

In the United Kingdom, over 53 million people are crowded into 93,895 square miles of territory. The resulting population density of about 563 per square mile is—after that of Belgium, the Netherlands, and West Germany—the heaviest in Europe. This population is highly urbanized, and the majority are employed in manufacturing industries, transportation, commerce, finance, and related industries. About 53% of Britain's land, which includes some of the best agricultural soil in the world, is under cultivation; the exact amount fluctuates from year to year. Another 25–30% is used for rough grazing land. Between 5 and 6% of the population are engaged in agriculture.

This situation developed over a period of two centuries, and the United Kingdom has come to recognize that its welfare depends primarily upon the success of its manufacturing industries and its overseas commerce. Approximately half of the total food supply has to be imported. This proportion can be sharply reduced, as it was in both World Wars, by plowing up grassland and shifting from animal husbandry to the growing of direct consumption crops. But this is not practicable under normal circumstances. Agriculture is directed toward the production of foodstuffs, such as dairy products, meat, eggs, and vegetables, whose relatively high value makes it profitable to produce them by intensive use of high-cost land.

The object of Britain's commercial policy is to maintain and increase the overseas sales of factory products. For this reason, the United Kingdom has viewed with some concern the success of the Common Market, which threatens to reduce British sales in Western Europe. The United Kingdom decided in 1961 to apply for membership in the Common Market rather than risk the economic consequences of virtual exclusion from the West European market. Discussions on the conditions of the United Kingdom's entry lasted many months, until they were terminated by the opposition of De Gaulle of France, who desired to see the Common Market restricted to the six countries of continental Western Europe.

Britain's restricted area, the growth of cities, and the competition for (and among) industry, mining, agriculture, and urban areas cause an internal problem. This problem is controlled—if not solved—by centralized planning of industrial location and land use. For example, a limit has been set on the growth of London, and the overflow from the metropolis is being accommodated in "new

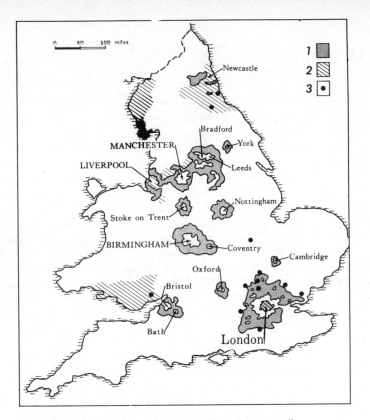

1–"green belt"; 2–"development area"; 3–"new town"

towns," located outside the greater London area. Around other large cities, separate "overspill" towns are being created.

Many parts of Great Britain, where factory industry developed during the period of the Industrial Revolution, are now derelict and partially abandoned. These areas are commonly coal fields which no longer attract industry as they did during the nineteenth century. These have been classified as "development areas," to which some new industries are attracted by government assistance.

The planned use of land also permits the protection of areas of natural beauty. "Green belts" have been established around some cities, and this practice is being continued. A number of national parks have been created. In these ways, the government has attempted to make the best use of its limited resources and to achieve some compromise between the competing demands for that scarcest of commodities, land.

16. Ireland

Ireland is one of the most compact and regular islands around the coast of Europe. It is separated from Great Britain by the stormy Irish Sea. The Irish people originally spoke Celtic, and their organization was tribal before the English attempted the conquest of Ireland during the Middle Ages. Most of the island was overrun and taken over by English landowners, but it was never really settled by people from Great Britain. Although a rather substantial number of Danes and Normans settled in southern Ireland, especially in the district around Dublin known as the Pale, they were largely assimilated by the Irish. The northern province of Ulster was an exception; it was the area least touched by English influence until the reign of Queen Elizabeth I, but as a result of a series of nationalist revolts she and her successors slaughtered or expelled most of the original population and colonized the area, largely with Presbyterian Scots, the ancestors of today's Ulstermen. Subsequently, there was a gradual drift of Catholic Irish from the south back to the north, so that many parts of historic Ulster again became predominantly Celtic.

The bulk of the Irish remained Catholic at the time of the Reformation—spurred, perhaps, by their own protest against Protestant England. Repeated revolts against British rule culminated in a civil war, and in 1921 the independence of "southern" Ireland within the British Commonwealth was recognized by the United Kingdom. By the terms of the treaty, the six northern counties (Antrim, Down, Armagh, Londonderry, Tyrone, and Fermanagh), which comprised about half of the ancient province of Ulster, were to be allowed to remain outside the Irish Free State if they wished. This they chose to do. Irish nationalists charged that the area chosen for self-determination was artificially gerrymandered, since it excluded parts of historic Ulster whose large nationalist majorities would have placed the result in doubt, while including other equally nationalist areas whose vote was certain to be outweighed by that of Protestant Belfast.

Northern Ireland is the most industrialized, developed, and wealthy segment of the island. Its economy is based on its linen and ship-building industries and its close association with Great Britain. A majority of the people of the counties of Tyrone and Fermanagh and of some districts in Antrim and Down favor union with "southern" Ireland, but the bulk of the population of the six counties taken as a whole are solidly "Unionist."

1 ANTRIM
2 ARMAGH
3 DOWN
4 FERMANAGH
5 LONDONDERRY
6 TYRONE

In 1949, the Irish Free State became the Republic of Eire and left the Commonwealth. It continues to enjoy a favored position in Great Britain for its farm produce and its casual and migratory labor. But the Republic refuses to enter into any alliance with Great Britain as long as the partition of Ireland continues, and it remains committed to the eventual unification of Ireland, although officially the government has renounced violence as a means.

17. Iceland

In area, Iceland is one of the largest states of Europe, but it is almost the smallest in population. Much of its 39,768 square miles is made up of bare rock and ice fields, and its natural vegetation consists mainly of low-growing Arctic species. Over 80 per cent of its area is totally unproductive, and since only about .5 per cent of its area can be cultivated, agriculture is restricted to hay and hardy root crops. (The remaining nonarable land is made up of rough grazing land for sheep.) Thermal springs furnish the chief domestic source of energy, and water is piped from them to heat the capital city of Reykjavík.

The wealth of Iceland lies in its fisheries. These provide the most important source of employment, and fish and fish products make up almost all of Iceland's exports. This overwhelming dependence on the fisheries, coupled with the danger that the North Atlantic fishing grounds might become overworked, helps to explain Iceland's recent extension of her territorial sea to 12 miles, measured from a baseline that links up the headlands along the Icelandic coast.

Most of the population of about 179,000, half of whom live in Reykjavík, are descended from the Norse settlers who went there from Norway during the ninth century and later. Their language is derived from Old Norse. For many centuries, Iceland was a sort of feudal republic, peopled by adventurers and refugees from Scandinavia and the Scandinavian kingdoms of Ireland and the western islands. It was conquered by the Norwegian Crown in 1264, and sovereignty passed to Denmark in 1280.

In 1918, Iceland became an independent monarchy, with the king of Denmark also serving as king of Iceland. In 1944, this relationship was dissolved, and Iceland became a republic.

Iceland owes much of its current importance to its location in the North Atlantic—near the shortest sea and air route between the northeastern United States and northwestern Europe. This importance has declined somewhat, now that fewer aircraft find it necessary to land at Iceland's airports for refueling, but it is unlikely to disappear. Iceland's location alone would continue to make it a significant member of NATO. For a while, Iceland enjoyed the unique distinction of being the only NATO member governed by a cabinet in which the Communist Party was represented. The American military base on the island is an important source of income to

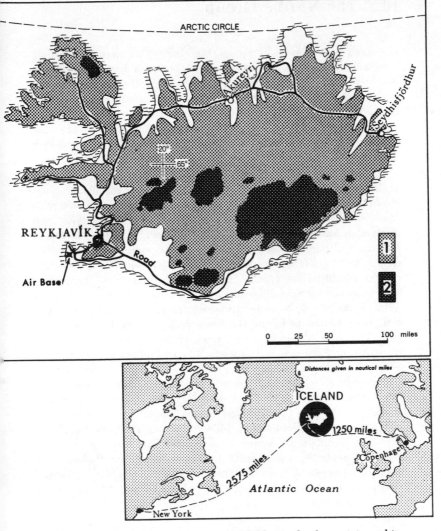

1—upland (largely unproductive); *2*—ice field. Much of remaining white area can be used for pastureland and fodder crops

the Icelanders, but the presence of the base is resented by many of the more nationalistic citizens.

18.   The Nordic Group

The three Scandinavian countries, together with Finland, have long been a distinct group among the nation-states of Europe. They are closely related culturally, and at various times each of the Scandinavian states has been linked politically with the others. Until 1809, Finland was a dependency of Sweden. The languages of Norway, Sweden, and Denmark are so closely related (*see Map 11*) that they are intelligible to natives in all three countries, and Swedish is the second language in Finland.

The lands of Norway, Sweden, and Finland are composed mainly of the hard, old rocks of the Scandinavian Shield; the mountainous terrain and the harsh climate limit the possibilities of agriculture in northern Sweden and Norway, but Denmark and the southern part of Sweden are prosperous agricultural areas. The natural wealth of Norway and northern Sweden lies in forests, mines, and the hydro-electric power obtained from their mountain streams. These circumstances condition the type of trade and the nature of the trading associations of the Scandinavian countries.

In World War I, Norway, Denmark, and Sweden remained neutral. They sought to follow the same policy in World War II, but only Sweden was able to do so, since Hitler refused to respect the neutrality of Denmark and Norway. On several occasions, the governments of the Scandinavian countries—each democratic, liberal, and progressive—have been able in the past to take joint action in international matters. But their unity of action has been somewhat shaken by the fact that Finland is now bound by the terms of a peace treaty not to join any anti-Soviet bloc; at the same time, Norway and Denmark are members of NATO, and Sweden pursues a policy of neutrality (or at least nonalignment). Nevertheless, since 1956 their representatives have been meeting in the Nordic Council to discuss closer coordination of their policies toward the major problems of the world.

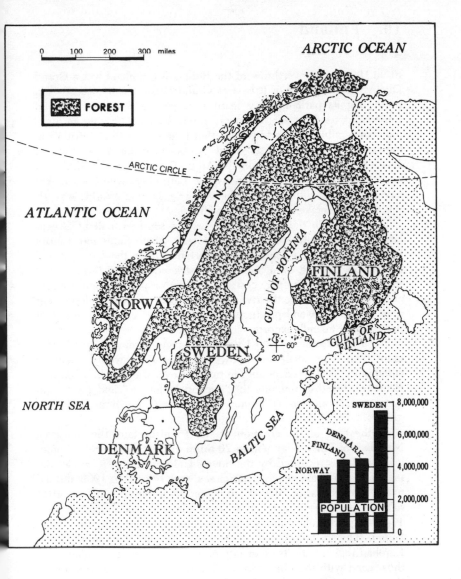

19.   Finland

From 1809 to the overthrow of the Romanovs, Finland was a Grand Duchy, with the Czar of Russia as Grand Duke, but it succeeded in preserving its parliamentary institutions and a degree of internal freedom. After the Czar was overthrown, Finland became an independent republic. The addition at that time of a strip of territory in the extreme north—the so-called Arctic Corridor—gave Finland access to an ice-free coast and the Arctic Ocean. (On the south and southwest, Finland is bordered by the Baltic Sea, where ice makes navigation impossible during the winter.) During World War II, this strip was retaken by the Soviet Union.

Finland lies in the same latitude as the southern half of Greenland. It is a country of coniferous forest, which fades into tundra toward the north. Agriculture is important only in the southern half of the country, and even there it is restricted to dairy farming and the raising of hay, fodder, cereal, and root crops. The only sources of industrial power are the rivers. The economy is heavily dependent upon wood and wood products, which together constitute some 42 per cent of Finland's exports.

The Finns speak a Finno-Ugrian language. A minority of slightly more than 8 per cent speak Swedish, but this Swedish-speaking community has been declining in number over the past half-century. However, Swedish remains the "second language," and public announcements and street names are generally given in both languages.

At the time of the creation of the Finnish state, the southeast boundary of Finland lay within 20 miles of the Soviet city of Leningrad, and was regarded by the Soviet Union as a threat. Soviet demands that Finland cede certain areas were refused in 1939 and led to the Winter War of 1939–40, followed by a second war from 1941 to 1944. As a result of the two wars, Finland was obliged to cede 17,024 square miles, almost 12 per cent of its area, to the Soviet Union. This included the Arctic Corridor and the industrialized Karelian region with its chief city of Viipuri (Viborg). Finland was thus faced with the obligation of finding new homes in the rest of the country for the more than 400,000 of its people who left the ceded area. Finland has since lived in the shadow of the Soviet Union, and until 1956 Soviet forces occupied the peninsula of Porkkala, which commands the entrance to the harbor of Helsinki, Finland's capital. Finland has participated in the Nordic Council and

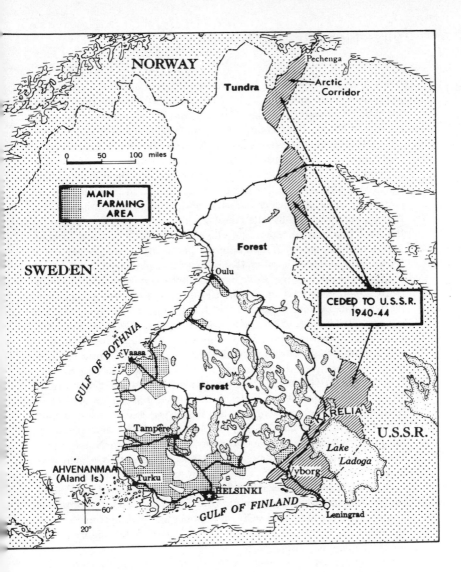

has requested closer association with the European Free Trade Association. But few important acts of policy are taken by Finland before consultation with the Soviet Union, and closer association between Finland and Western Europe seems unlikely.

20. Norway and Sweden

Norway and Sweden have long been closely associated. Norway was joined in a personal union with Sweden from 1814 until 1905, when the union was peacefully dissolved and the modern state of Norway came into being. Both countries are mountainous, with large areas of nonarable and forested land. In Norway, the fisheries, the merchant marine, and industries based upon hydroelectric power are important; Norwegian agriculture supplies about a third of the country's food, plus some dairy products for export. In Sweden, manufacturing—especially heavy industry—and mining and lumbering are important; agriculturally, the country is more or less self-sufficient in the food products of temperate climates. Although not comparable in size to the Norwegian merchant marine, whose earnings pay for a third of the country's imports, that of Sweden is also large.

Close commercial ties exist between both countries and Western Europe, and both have joined the European Free Trade Association. Norway and Denmark plan to join the European Common Market if Great Britain becomes a member (*see Map 60*), but Sweden's traditional policy of neutrality has thus far restrained her from taking a similar step. The important West German steel industry is a heavy user of Swedish ore, much of which is shipped from the ore fields in northern Sweden through the ice-free Norwegian port of Narvik. The abundance of hydroelectric power has encouraged electrochemical and electro-engineering industries, and Sweden is particularly noted for high-quality steel and electrical and precision machines, which she supplies to many countries. Both Norway and Sweden have in the past been important markets for German and Polish coal, but coal imports to Sweden are declining as the use of hydroelectric power increases. (This has made it difficult for Poland to purchase much-needed iron ore from Sweden.) The northern half of Sweden is forested, and softwood lumber and products made from it (pulpwood, plywood, and even prefabricated homes) figure prominently among Swedish exports.

Both countries have been notable for their extremely stable and progressive governments and for their freedom from both internal strife and external conflict. Sweden, in particular, has adopted a highly successful planned and socially oriented economy, sometimes described as the "middle way." Sweden also has a state-operated medical system.

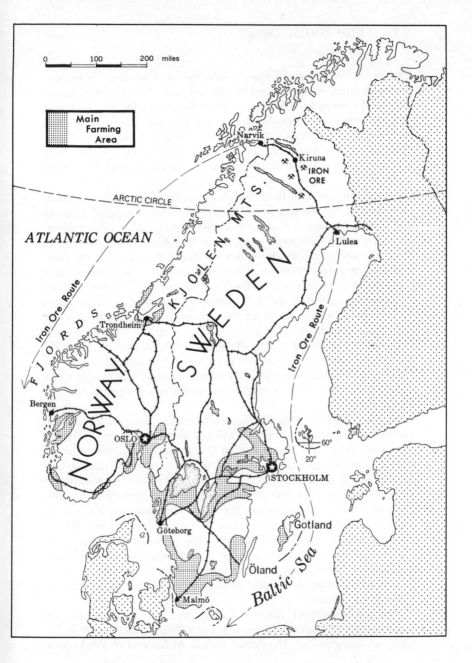

21. The Baltic Sea

The Baltic Sea is part of the division between Western and Communist Europe. It is bordered on the southeast by the Soviet Union and on the south by Poland and East Germany. On the northeast and northwest (respectively) lie neutral Finland and Sweden. Only on the west, where there is access from the Baltic Sea to the North Sea through the Danish Straits and the Kiel Canal, are there any countries fully committed to the West (Denmark and West Germany).

Three centuries ago, the Baltic Sea was not so divided; the whole of it formed, in effect, a Swedish lake. Sweden controlled Finland and also had possessions along the southeastern and southern shore. But early in the eighteenth century, Prussia drove the Swedes from their foothold on the southern shore of the Baltic. Toward the east, Sweden lost a struggle to check the expansion of Czarist Russia, and Czar Peter the Great seized the head of the Gulf of Finland. In 1703, he founded the city of St. Petersburg (now Leningrad), and he later occupied the whole of the east coast of the Baltic Sea. At the end of World War I, Russia, then in the throes of the Bolshevik Revolution, lost control of the whole eastern coast of the Baltic, with the sole exception of the head of the Gulf of Finland and the city of Leningrad. The four republics of Finland, Estonia, Latvia, and Lithuania came into existence after a successful revolt against the new Soviet Union.

At the same time, Poland reappeared on the map with a narrow corridor that gave her access to the sea and to the port of Danzig (Gdansk). The new map reflected the weakened political position of the Soviet Union and Germany. But this power relationship was soon changed. During the 1930's, the Soviet Union grew steadily in economic and military strength. After the signing of the Hitler-Stalin Pact, the Soviet Union made territorial demands on Finland in 1939, which Finland acquiesced to only as a result of the Winter War of 1939–40. In 1941, Finland, siding with Germany, declared war on the Soviet Union in the hope of regaining some of her losses. Finland was again defeated, lost a small additional area, and was required by the Second Treaty of Moscow to pay a large indemnity to the Soviet Union.

The Baltic states of Estonia, Latvia, and Lithuania succumbed more easily to Soviet demands—first for military bases and then for their incorporation into the Soviet Union. At the end of World War

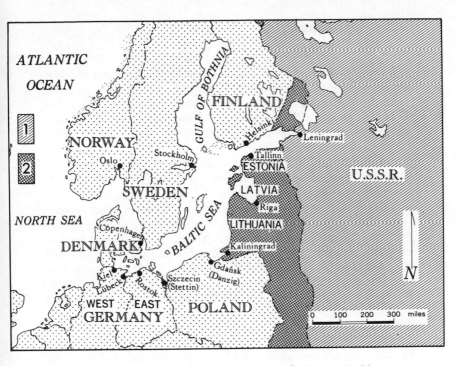

1—Soviet territory before 1939; 2—Soviet territorial gains, 1939–45

II, the Soviet Union acquired the northern part of East Prussia (formerly a German province) with its port of Königsberg (now Kaliningrad). The Russians thus became more firmly established on the shore of the Baltic Sea than at any time in their history.

Access to the Baltic Sea from the west is gained through either the Kiel Canal, opened in 1895 across the base of the Danish peninsula, or through the Danish Straits. Of the latter, the Sound, between the Danish island of Sjaelland and the Swedish mainland, is by far the most important.

22. Denmark

Since it first appeared as an independent kingdom during the Middle Ages, Denmark has been the guardian of the straits that lead from the Baltic Sea into the Kattegat, Skagerrak, and North Sea. Denmark consists of the peninsula of Jutland (Jylland) and a large number of islands, of which Fyn, Sjaelland, and Lolland are the largest and most important. Until 1658, Denmark had possession of the coastal region of southern Sweden. Denmark continues to include the island of Bornholm, lying in the Baltic Sea 90 miles to the east of Sjaelland.

Three waterways lead from the Baltic into the Kattegat and on to the North Sea: the Little Belt, the Great Belt, and the Sound. Navigation of the first two is difficult because of narrow, winding channels between the Danish islands. The last-named, the Sound, is the most easily navigated and most often used. At its narrowest point, it is less than 3 miles across, and at this point the Danish Government for many years exacted a toll from every passing ship, until the tolls were abolished by an international agreement in 1857.

On the shores of the Sound lie the Danish port of Copenhagen and the Swedish port of Malmö. The right of free navigation of the Danish Straits is now guaranteed by treaty, but Denmark is still the guardian of the straits and could again close this outlet from the Baltic, as she has done in the past. Apart from the commerce of Sweden and Finland, the ships that pass through the Danish Straits belong almost entirely to the Baltic countries of the Communist bloc.

Denmark is an agricultural country, but it also has important manufacturing industries. During the nineteenth century, Danish agriculture was revolutionized, and with the help of cooperatives for processing and marketing, Danish farmers began to concentrate on dairying. Farm produce, most of it meat and dairy produce, makes up a little more than half of the total exports. The market for Danish farm produce is mainly in Western Europe.

A constitutional monarchy, Denmark has an elected Parliament, or Folketing. The largest party in the Folketing is the Social Democrats, a socialist party which does not have a clear majority. The government is a coalition in which Social Democrats predominate.

Strategic location and commerce have been important influences on Danish foreign policy, leading Denmark to join NATO and also to join Britain in seeking membership in the European Common Market.

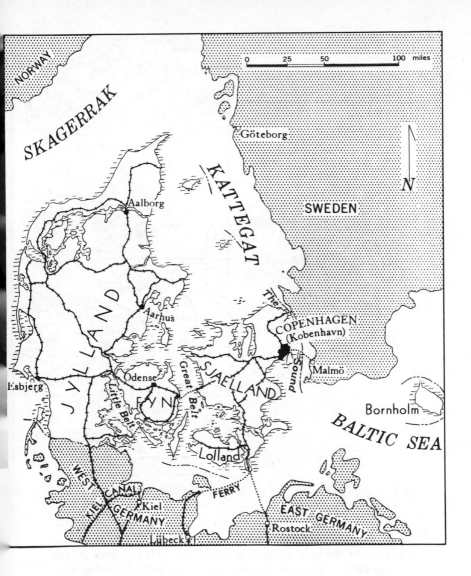

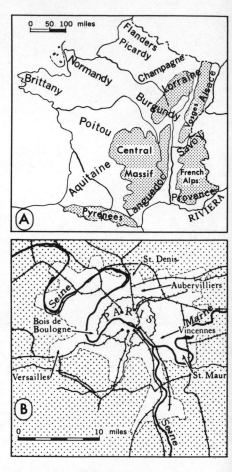

A. *Selected regional names and major highland areas*
B. *Greater Paris*
C. *Mineral deposits and industry: 1—coal; 2—iron ore; 3—major industrial region*

23. France

Despite the appearances of political confusion, France is in many ways one of the most stable states in Europe. It has both industry and agriculture, a variety of resources, and a high degree of homogeneity in its culture. The boundaries of France have changed little for a century and a half. Alsace-Lorraine was lost in 1871 and regained in 1919, Savoy and Nice were acquired from Italy in 1860, and some small areas were gained in the French Alps in 1947.

Almost the whole population, at present about 46 million, speak French. German is spoken in Alsace-Lorraine, Basque in the Pyre-

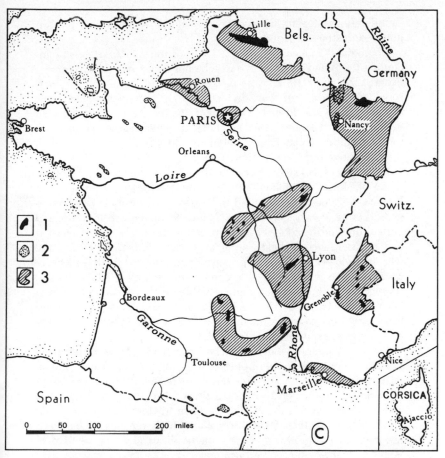

nees, Arabic and the languages of Eastern Europe in Paris and other cities, and Italian and Spanish near the borders of Italy and Spain. France has no pressing minority problems, although provincial feeling is strong in Brittany, Provence, and elsewhere.

France's government is one of the most centralized in Europe. In part, this high degree of centralization was created deliberately to overcome the centrifugal tendencies of the ancient provinces of France. During the French Revolutionary period (1789–94), these provinces were replaced, for purposes of administration, by more than eighty *départements* (the number has since increased). These were wholly artificial divisions; most of them were named for mountains or rivers, and their creation was intended to symbolize the break with the past. It has proved difficult, however, to eradicate

47

completely the feeling among the provincials of belonging to Burgundy or Brittany or Aquitaine.

Continental France today is made up of ninety *départements,* including the island of Corsica (which constitutes one *département*). From 1881 until 1962, Algeria was regarded as a part of metropolitan France and was divided into *départements* that were represented in the French Parliament up to the time of Algerian independence (August, 1962). There are "overseas *départements*" for Martinique, Guadeloupe, Réunion, and Guiana, each of which is represented in the French Parliament.

By reason of its extent, its rich and varied resources, and its population of almost 46 million, France is one of the strongest states in Europe, both economically and militarily. This position was endangered before World War II by a failure to modernize industry and agriculture and by too great a respect for the traditional ways that had made France a great nation a century earlier. Following the war, in 1946–47, a plan was prepared and adopted for the modernization of the whole French economy—the so-called Monnet Plan. Its success was in large part made possible by over $5 billion of direct aid received from the United States under the Marshall Plan and other programs, as well as further substantial U.S. assistance through such devices as offshore procurement.

During this period, much progress has been made in modernizing French agriculture, in equipping it with modern machines, and in introducing new methods. This has been reflected in an increase of agricultural production to about a third more than the 1938 level and in the increase in the number of farm tractors from about 2,000 in 1946 to more than 80,000 in 1959. Much remains to be done, however, in the grouping of peasant holdings and the creation of larger and more manageable farm units.

Manufacturing has been revolutionized. New factories have been established, and many of the older ones have been either modernized or scrapped. The change has been particularly apparent in the heavy industries. Steel production has increased to twice the 1929 level.

France imports substantial quantities of coal in addition to her own production but has abundant resources in hydroelectric power, and her iron-ore reserves are the largest in Europe. Modern industries have arisen beside the traditional quality industries for which France has always been known. This careful planning for the development of resources has been a triumph for France.

France's most important problem has long been her relations with her eastern neighbor. A generation ago, or even in the late 1940's, one would have said that the whole of France's foreign policy was shaped by the supreme need to protect herself against Germany. This has changed radically in recent years, and hostility and fear have been replaced by friendship and collaboration between the two. A major factor in this change has undoubtedly been the fact that both France and Germany see in the Soviet Union a danger that overshadows their own differences. The success of the Coal and Steel Community (*see Map 58*), followed by the even greater achievement of the Common Market, has demonstrated the advantages of free trade and economic and technical collaboration within Western Europe. France willingly relinquished her claim to the Saar (*see Map 31a*), and West Germany has also made concessions to this new *entente cordiale*.

France's most important external problem has been the management of her overseas territories and dependencies. The French Empire was once second only to the British in extent. In the past, French policy never conceived of a gradual granting of freedom and independence to these possessions; rather, it aimed to make them French in language and culture. It was successful only in a few small and relatively unimportant areas, now the overseas *départements* of France. It failed in Southeast Asia and Africa, where the French were ultimately obliged to recognize that the vast majority of the people wanted nothing more than to run their own affairs in their own fashion. All these parts of the former empire are now independent, although many former African possessions are still closely tied to France economically and militarily, and French technicians and advisers still play key roles in their governments. In Algeria, the situation was made more complex by the settlement of the French *colons* and the admission of the northern *départements* of Algeria as integral parts of France. Out of a total population of more than 10 million, about 1 million (10 per cent) were French. The remainder were ethnically North African or Berber, and their religion Moslem. In 1954, the Berbers, demanding independence for Algeria, rose in revolt against the French. In 1962, their struggle finally won them independence, and Algeria was proclaimed a republic.

The Algerian situation was largely responsible for the fall of the Fourth Republic, which had been established by the constitution of 1946, and for the establishment of the Fifth. As a result of a military revolt, General de Gaulle, the Free French military leader of World War II, took office in June, 1958, with emergency powers both to deal with the Algerian situation and to reform the constitution. In the following September, his draft constitution was accepted by the electorate by a large majority, and the Fifth Republic was born. The new constitution gives exceptional powers to the President, who can

49

nominate and dismiss the Prime Minister, dissolve the National Assembly, and take whatever measures are demanded by the circumstances to ensure the continuity of the Republic and the maintenance of public order. The position of the President has been further strengthened by a constitutional amendment that shifts the power to elect him from the National Assembly to a direct vote of the people. De Gaulle continues to serve as President, and Prime Minister Pompidou and Foreign Minister Couve de Murville do little more than execute his policies.

24. Benelux Union

In 1944, the governments of Belgium, the Netherlands, and Luxembourg signed a treaty by which they established a customs union. Belgium had, in fact, already created such a union with the Grand Duchy of Luxembourg in 1922, and the Netherlands and the Belgium-Luxembourg Union began to remove the obstacles to trade among them by 1948.

In some respects, this was a reversion to a late medieval pattern, which had been interrupted by the revolt of the Dutch at the end of the sixteenth century and had been temporarily re-created from 1815 to 1830. Despite their common heritage, however, the Dutch and Belgians had become bitter rivals, and it proved difficult to overcome their deep-seated opposition to one another. In particular, the two Dutch ports of Rotterdam and Amsterdam competed with the Belgian ports of Antwerp and Ghent, whose access to the sea is through Dutch territorial waters. In fact, the Dutch succeeded in closing the port of Antwerp for most of the seventeenth and eighteenth centuries, to the great advantage of Amsterdam.

Although they are individually small, the Benelux nations together make up a market of about 21 million people. With a market potential of this size, it is possible to establish industries that would not be practicable in a smaller state. The three countries are not wholly complementary in their economies, although Belgium tends to be engaged more in manufacturing, and the Netherlands in agriculture, while the economy of Luxembourg is based on steel production.

At the time of Union, there proved to be many areas in which Belgium and the Netherlands were competing. For example, vegetables and other types of produce were in general grown more

cheaply in the Netherlands than in Belgium, and it was impossible to remove the trade barriers all at once without doing serious harm to Belgian industry, which had previously been highly protected. Nevertheless, initial difficulties have, to a considerable extent, been overcome.

51

25. Belgium and Luxembourg

Belgium was originally that part of the broad region of the Low Countries that the Spaniards were able to reconquer and hold after the revolts that broke out there late in the sixteenth century. The boundary line was, in general, determined by the course of the fighting. What was to become Belgium remained under Spanish rule until 1713, then passed to Austria; it was reunited with the Netherlands in 1815 and did not become an independent state until 1830. These changes have hindered the growth of a Belgian national tradition and sense of cohesion, which most other countries of Western Europe have.

Belgium is divided into two almost equal halves by a linguistic line running roughly from west to east through Brussels. The people of the northern region speak Flemish, which as a written language is the same as Dutch, and in the southern region Walloon, a French dialect, is spoken. Rivalry between these two has sometimes been bitter, and recently (1962) it again became acute. In the early years of the Belgian state, it was the Walloons who constituted the dominant group. Because of the higher Flemish birthrate, the Walloons have now become a minority, but are still culturally more influential because of the greater prestige of the French language. The cultural differences are still emphasized by differences in political, religious, and social attitudes.

Belgium is an important manufacturing state, with coal-mining, iron and steel, and textile industries. The Belgian coal field has been worked a long time, and many of its mines are old and costly to operate. This, and the fact that a number of the mines had to be closed, made Belgium's participation in the Coal and Steel Community difficult.

The chief Belgian port is Antwerp, on the River Scheldt. Ships reach Antwerp only after sailing through Dutch waters. Antwerp aspires to become a port serving the Rhineland, but the waterways linking it with the Rhineland are circuitous, and a canal, projected to join Antwerp directly to the Rhine, still has not been built.

The Grand Duchy of Luxembourg is one of the smallest states in Europe and has a population of only about 317,000. It was created in 1867, when a larger state of Luxembourg was divided, along approximately linguistic lines. The more westerly, French-speaking part of Luxembourg was absorbed into Belgium. The remainder—primarily German-speaking—became the Grand Duchy. Until World

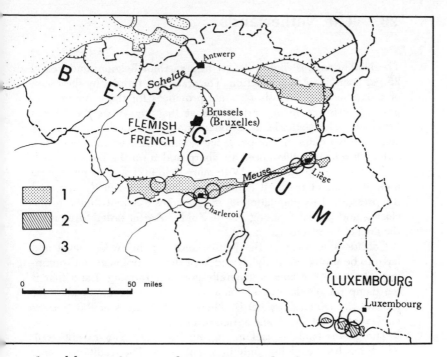

1—coal deposits; *2*—iron-ore deposits; *3*—iron and steel center

War I, it was in a customs union with Germany. In 1922 it entered into a similar union with Belgium.

Although Luxembourg is primarily an agricultural country, it has one important industry. Across its southern margin lies an extension of the great iron-ore deposits of eastern France, and on these deposits has been based Luxembourg's iron and steel industry. The iron-ore deposits are now becoming exhausted, and Luxembourg will soon be obliged to rely on ore imported from neighboring Lorraine. Luxembourg has always imported its coke and coal, most of it from West Germany.

Luxembourg is heavily dependent upon the export of iron and steel goods. Although she has many advantages that prompt her to continue her iron and steel industries, her neighbors have similar industries, and she has to sell in competition with them. For this reason, Luxembourg derives great benefits from its membership in the Coal and Steel Community, whose headquarters is in the city of Luxembourg.

26.   The Netherlands

The Netherlands is slightly larger in area than Belgium and nearly 25 per cent larger in population. The state was formed by the union of a number of previously separate provinces for the common purpose of resisting Spain, and it was at first known as the United Provinces. The Netherlands is today one of the most homogeneous and cohesive states in Europe. It has no important ethnic minorities, although religious differences are sharp and form the basis of much of the country's political life. With more than 900 persons per square mile, it is one of the most densely populated states in Europe, and the pressure of its population on its resources has contributed to the closing and partial draining of the Zuider Zee in order to increase the area of farmland.

Considerable areas of the Netherlands are below sea level and have to be protected by dykes and kept dry by drainage and pumping. The low-lying land is generally good for farming. Land that is too damp for regular cultivation is commonly used as meadow for grazing the Dutch dairy herds. There are few areas of the Netherlands that do not have some agricultural value.

The Netherlands is lacking in mineral resources—except coal, which has been exploited only in recent years. The traditional function of the Dutch has been to serve as intermediaries in the commerce of Europe, and their geographical location has aided them in this role. The Rhine (*see Map 29*), the chief avenue of commerce in West Germany, enters the sea through the Netherlands. The port of Rotterdam, whose efficiency was improved by the construction of the New Waterway linking it to the sea, transships much of West Germany's trade in bulk goods, such as coal, iron ore, lumber, and grain. Amsterdam, not as well suited for river-borne trade with Germany, handles only a small part of West Germany's maritime commerce, but is very important in the domestic trade of the Netherlands.

The accident of boundary delimitation in the seventeenth century left the Netherlands with two extensions of territory, which in the past greatly hampered the development of neighboring Belgium. One is the westward extension across the river Scheldt, between Antwerp and the sea; the other is the Limburg extension southeastward between Belgium and Germany. The former gave the Dutch a stranglehold on the commerce of their rival port, Antwerp—an advantage that they did not hesitate to use at one time. However,

1—land below sea level; *2*—coal deposits

on May 13, 1963, the Dutch and the Belgian governments signed a treaty that permits construction of a canal from Antwerp across the Netherlands to The Hague, giving Belgium access to the North Sea.

27. Germany

The German Empire was created in 1871 by the union of a large number of states, most of them small and weak. The Germany that went to war in 1914 covered an area more than twice the size of the present Federal Republic and included in its population (almost 56 million) a large Polish minority, a substantial French population in Alsace-Lorraine, and a smaller Danish population in Schleswig. The German republic that emerged from World War I was shorn of Alsace-Lorraine in the west, North Schleswig, and large areas in the east that formed part of the new Poland (*see Map 36*). It was divided into two parts by the so-called Polish Corridor, which reached down to the Baltic coast and separated East Prussia from the rest of Germany.

In 1933, Adolf Hitler, the leader of the National Socialists, came to power, abolished the Weimar Republic, and established one of the most powerful totalitarian regimes in history. Under Hitler, the Nazis soon began to carry out a policy of aggression and conquest that had been gradually taking shape in Germany for several years. The Saarland was returned to Germany by an internationally conducted plebiscite held in accordance with the terms of the Treaty of Versailles, and the Memel territory was reincorporated into the Reich. Austria was annexed (1938), the Sudetenland of Czechoslovakia (*see Map 34*) was occupied, and the rest of Czechoslovakia was reduced to a tributary status. Hitler's invasion of Poland precipitated World War II in September, 1939.

The territorial changes resulting from Germany's defeat in 1945 were more drastic than those that followed World War I. All territory east of the Oder and the Neisse rivers was incorporated into Poland, together with the port of Stettin (now Szczecin), which lies on the west bank of the Oder. (These changes have not yet been confirmed by an international treaty, and they are regarded as legal and binding only by the countries of the Communist bloc.) Certain very small areas, totaling only 36 square miles, were taken from Germany for technical reasons by the Netherlands, Belgium, Luxembourg, and France. By mutual consent, some small exchanges of territory to rectify frontiers later took place between Germany and the Netherlands. Lastly, Germany was divided, for purposes of Allied occupation, into four zones, with the city of Berlin (also divided into four sectors) lying entirely within the Eastern (or Soviet-held) zone. This division was regarded as only temporary, and was

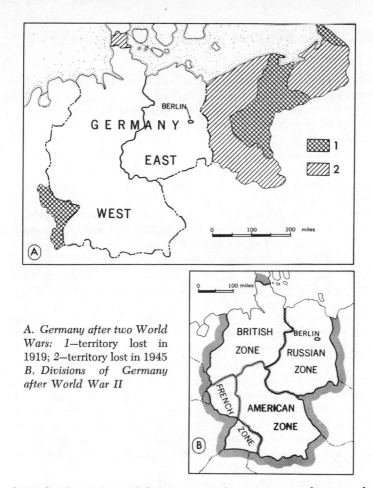

A. *Germany after two World Wars:* 1—territory lost in 1919; 2—territory lost in 1945
B. *Divisions of Germany after World War II*

planned to last only until the signature of a peace treaty between the wartime allies and Germany.

The Federal Republic of Germany derives from the three Western occupation zones of Germany. The original American and British zones were merged economically in 1947, and they were joined by the French zone in 1948. Political and economic restrictions on the German people were gradually eased, and in 1949 the Federal Republic of Germany was established. In 1951, the Western powers formally terminated the state of war with Germany, and in 1955 the Occupation Statute was revoked, and the Federal Republic became a sovereign and independent state.

28. The Federal Republic of Germany

The West German state adopted a federal constitution, in part because the historical tradition and the strength of local feeling favored this form of government, and in part because the Allied powers were suspicious of a strong unitary government. The Federal Republic of Germany (Bundesrepublik Deutschland) at first consisted of nine *Länder,* but a clause in its constitution permitted the accession of other areas that had once been Germany. On January 1, 1957, the Saarland became the tenth *Länd.* While a liberated East Germany could easily be fitted into the present constitutional structure of the Federal Republic, leaders of all major parties made it clear that the constitution is subject to revision in a unified Germany. West Berlin is not a part of the Federal Republic, though it is closely associated with it. It is represented in the Bundesrat, or Council of States, the upper house of the Federal Parliament, and elects nonvoting members to the Bundestag, the lower house. Berliners may hold federal office, and have served in West German cabinets. And some departments of the West German government have offices in Berlin. Two of the *Länder* consist of the cities of Hamburg and Bremen, with their surrounding areas.

The duties and obligations of the German federal government are enumerated in the Basic Law (or Constitution) and include foreign policy, defense, immigration, currency, postal services, and certain other functions. Those not enumerated are the responsibility of the local governments of the *Länder.* Bonn was chosen as the federal capital because at that time it was thought to be one of the very few undamaged cities that could offer the accommodations and amenities required by the government.

The economic unity of Germany had developed during a period of over a century. Germany was gradually knit together by railroads, roads, and canals. Agricultural and industrial specialization grew up within Germany, and the products of each region or locality were distributed to all others. The territorial changes that resulted from World War I made little difference in this pattern of trade and exchange. After World War II, however, Germany was split three ways. The most easterly sector was absorbed into Poland and the Soviet Union, and the rest of the country was divided into West and East Germany.

These changes had two important consequences. First, refugees from the areas occupied by Poland, as well as German refugees

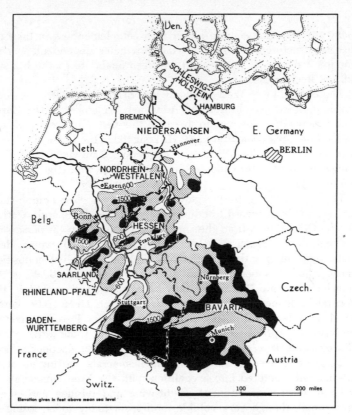

Elevation given in feet above mean sea level

from Czechoslovakia and other Danubian and Balkan countries, fled westward. Altogether, the Federal Republic received over 12 million, and at least one person out of every five was a refugee. Second, the separation of West from East Germany, which hindered trade between them, broke up the earlier pattern of specialization and exchange. Very broadly, West Germany had most of the coal-mining, steel, heavy engineering, and cotton-textile industries; East Germany had a large part of the electrical manufacturing, optical and other precision and light engineering, chemical, and woolen-textile industries. Many East German industries were dependent on highly skilled workers, and the mass flight of the latter to the West resulted in the transfer of much of the output of these industries from East to West.

Within each of the two Germanies since World War II, much of the industrial growth has been aimed at replacing the industries lost because of the division. The result is that now East and West Germany are becoming similar, rather than complementary, in their industrial structures. But East Germany remains dependent on coal imports, having only lignite, and has been unable to establish a significant steel industry.

The Basic Law of West Germany was drafted in 1949 by a committee presided over by Konrad Adenauer, a member of the Christian Democratic Union who became the first Chancellor of the Federal Republic soon afterward. He resigned in the fall of 1963, and was succeeded by his Minister of Economics, Ludwig Erhard. The Christian Democratic Union's supporters range from the moderate left to the far right.

They are held together largely by a desire for close church-state ties, especially in regard to education. While predominantly Catholic, the CDU differs from the pre-Hitler Center Party in possessing a significant Protestant wing. Its Protestant support, however, fluctuates more sharply than its Catholic backing. The chief opposition party, which has been gaining ground in recent elections, is the Social Democratic Party. The only other party represented in the Federal Parliament, or Bundestag, is the Free Democratic Party, which includes old-fashioned liberals like former President Heuss, conservative representatives of big business, and some ultra-nationalist elements. It received enough votes in the 1962 elections to hold a balance of power, and the Christian Democrats, lacking an absolute majority, entered into a coalition with the Free Democrats in order to form a government. Right-wing and refugee parties are quite small, though very voluble, and seem today to be losing in importance. The Communist Party was declared illegal in 1961.

29. The Rhine

Among the transportation facilities that have aided in the dispersion of factory industry over all of West Germany is the Rhine. The river rises in Switzerland and becomes navigable for large river craft at the Swiss port of Basel. It leaves Swiss territory after Basel and for 110 miles forms the boundary between France and Germany. Then it flows across West Germany for more than 300 miles, enters the Netherlands, and empties into the sea. The tributaries of the Rhine are not naturally navigable for more than a short distance, but improvements have opened up the Main and Neckar rivers to navigation, and an agreement reached between France and the Federal

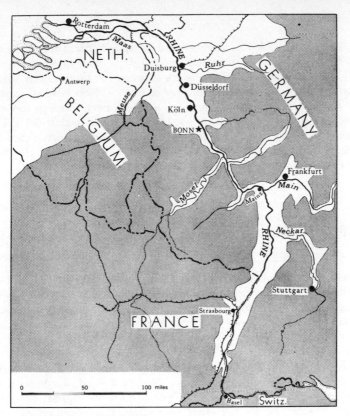

Highland areas are stippled

Republic of Germany in 1956 provided for the improvement of the Moselle River. Within the Netherlands, the Rhine breaks up into a number of navigable branches, which link the river with the many ports of the Low Countries.

Canals have been dug to link the lower Rhine to the Ems River and from there eastward to the Elbe River and to Berlin. Work is now in progress on an improved waterway from the Rhine, via the Main, to the Danube. Waterways in the Netherlands link the Rhine not only with its principal ocean port, Rotterdam, but also with Amsterdam and Antwerp, and the Dortmund-Ems Canal joins the Rhine and the Ruhr industrial region with the port of Emden.

The Rhine is one of the most heavily used rivers in the world. Much of West Germany's coal, iron ore, grain, lumber, and other bulky commodities are transported by way of the Rhine system and its linking canals.

The Rhine is also an international river, and it was the first ever to be subjected to international control. It is open to the traffic of all riparian states, and no tolls are charged for its use. The Rhine forms part of the eastern boundary of France. Napoleon attempted to establish France's boundary on the Rhine from Basel to the sea, but with his downfall France was forced to abandon this claim. The new spirit existing between Germany and France is exemplified by their agreement to improve the Moselle and to use it for the shipping of coal and iron ore between the Ruhr and Lorraine.

30. Berlin

When Berlin became the capital of the German Empire in 1871, it began a period of rapid growth as both an industrial city and a seat of government. To many Germans, the city typified a Prussian tradition to which they were far from sympathetic, but as the capital city of the German Empire it was the focus of their loyalties. Since the division and occupation of Germany in 1945 were regarded as only temporary at the time, it was assumed that Germany, with the possible exception of the areas occupied by Poland, would soon be reunited and that Berlin would again become its capital. The control of Berlin was thus of great importance, and it was agreed that control should be shared by the Soviet Union, Great Britain, the United States, and France.

Thus, Berlin was divided into four sectors for occupation by each of the four Allied powers. The right of the three Western powers to access to Berlin was guaranteed, but the terms of this agreement were never spelled out. The fortunes of Berlin have mirrored those of Germany. As the division between East and West Germany became more pronounced, so the city came to be divided also into East and West Berlin, each with its own city government. But it remained possible to move fairly freely between the two (until the Wall was built in August, 1961), and Berlin thus became an important escape route from East to West.

East German and Soviet interference with the supply route to West Berlin in 1948 led to the Allied airlift, which brought provisions to the city for eleven months, until the blockade was lifted. West Berlin was never regarded as a viable unit. It has a population of 2,198,000 and virtually no agricultural or mineral resources. All

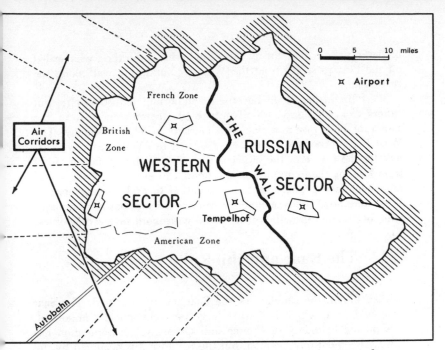

food and raw materials must be brought in from the West; hence the overwhelming importance of keeping open the supply routes.

The access routes to West Berlin are by road, rail, canal, and air. Certain railroads and roads are designated as access routes, and the traveler can usually get to Berlin across Germany's East Zone without undue delay or inconvenience. Occasionally, the Russian and East German authorities decide to be formal—to search trucks and freight cars and examine travelers' documents with obstructive meticulousness.

The canal route is along the Mittelland Canal; it is used by large barges and is very important for the supply of bulky materials. Aircraft have three narrow corridors which converge from West Germany on West Berlin. Normally, they are used for mail, lightweight freight, and escapees (since there is no ground control of the flights by the East German authorities).

The Western occupation of Berlin is a political gesture. It is maintained partly out of loyalty to the West Berliners, but mainly because it would be disastrous to withdraw in the face of Soviet pressure. West Berlin is an economic liability because of its complete dependence on West Germany for almost all its foodstuffs and raw materials and for the sale of most of its products.

On August 13, 1961, what vestiges still remained of a unified city of Berlin were wiped out by the East Berlin authorities, who sealed off the Eastern sector from the West by building a wall along the sector line.

West Berlin has again become an important industrial city, but suffers from the grave disadvantage of its remoteness from the source of both raw materials and markets in West Germany. The West Berlin economy has to be subsidized by West Germany. Anxiety for the future of the city has sometimes deterred industrialists from locating there, and it has also tended to drive the younger and more energetic sections of the population to seek employment in West Germany. The economic recovery of the city has been remarkable, but further growth will be faced with more severe difficulties.

31.   The Saar and the Ruhr

Unlike Berlin, the problem of the Saar has been solved. The Saar coal-field area, which is neither large nor economically important, lies on the boundary of France and Germany. Its population has always been entirely German, but the territory was occupied by the French during the Napoleonic Wars. It was again claimed by them at the end of World War I, in part as compensation for the destruction of the coal mines in northern France by the Germans, and in part because it had once been French. In the end, France obtained a fifteen-year lease on the coal field, while the government of the Saarland was placed under the League of Nations.

In 1935, after a plebiscite, the territory and the mines reverted to Germany. After 1945, the Saarland fell within the French zone of occupation, and the French again tried to detach the area and absorb it into France. In this they failed, and, as part of the agreement reached between France and Germany in 1956, the territory was again restored to Germany. On January 1, 1957, it became the tenth *Land* in the Federal Republic. The French had assumed that the coal of the Saar coal field would be used in the Lorraine iron-smelting industry, only 30 miles away. This did not, in fact, happen, as the Saar coal in general is not suitable as a metallurgical fuel and has been used for this purpose only on a very small scale.

The economic significance of the Saarland is minor when compared with the immense importance of the Ruhr. The Ruhr is the largest and most productive coal field in Europe; it contains the greatest variety of types of coal and supports the most powerful concentration of iron and steel industries in the continent. The Ruhr

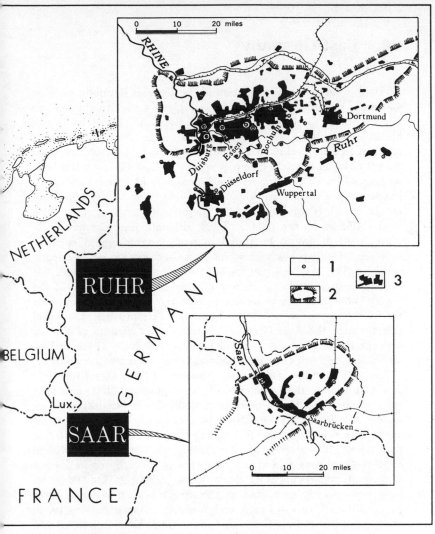

1—steel mill; 2—limit of coal field; 3—built-up area

is the heart of the German economy and has often been regarded as the mainspring of German militarism. It was occupied by the French in 1923 in an attempt to enforce the payment of reparations by Germany. After 1945, part of its industrial capacity was dismantled, and the rest was strictly controlled by an Allied commission. The industries have now been rebuilt and extended, and the productivity and importance of the Ruhr are greater today than ever before.

32. East Germany

In 1949, soon after the formation of the Federal Republic in West Germany, the Soviet-occupied zone was given a constitution and was declared to be the German Democratic Republic (Deutsche Demokratische Republik). East Germany is a unitary state with its government in East Berlin. In 1952 its *Länder* were replaced by fourteen *Bezirke*, or districts. The new regime in East Germany has been recognized by all countries of the Communist bloc and Yugoslavia, but it has not gained any diplomatic recognition in the non-Communist world. It thus is unable to conduct direct negotiations with most countries on the political level, although East German trade representatives are to be found in many countries and consular representatives in a few with which East Germany has no diplomatic relations. The Western powers insist on dealing directly with the Russian authorities in all matters relating to East Germany. If the Soviet Union makes a peace treaty with the Democratic Republic, the Western powers will be obliged, the Russians assert, to deal directly with the East German Government in matters of mutual concern (such as access to Berlin), since technically there will be no Russian authorities in East Germany with whom to negotiate.

East Germany has less than half the area of the Federal Republic and a little more than a quarter of the population. It is somewhat less industrialized than the Federal Republic. It has lost approximately 2 million of its population, predominantly from the younger age groups, who fled through Berlin to the West and the population that remains is relatively old. The Democratic Republic has tried to solve the problems arising from shortage of labor by collectivizing agriculture and regimenting the workers. Manufacturing industries have been greatly expanded in accordance with a series of state plans. Although rich in lignite and in certain mineral salts useful in chemical industry, East Germany has very little bituminous coal and iron ore, and it is very poorly located for many branches of industry compared to West Germany. East Germany was formerly served by the ports of Hamburg, now in West Germany, and Stettin, now in Poland. Thus it is currently developing Rostock as its chief maritime outlet.

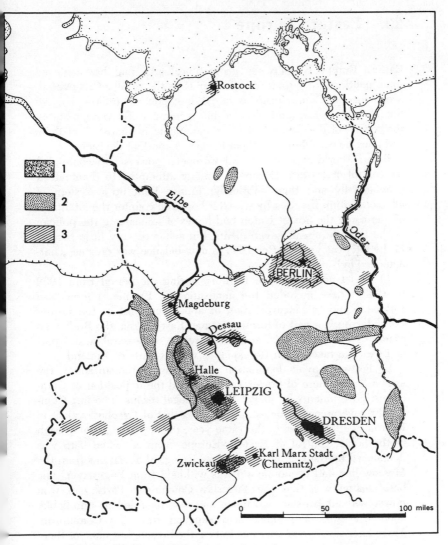

1—coal deposits; 2—lignite deposits; 3—industrial area

33. Eastern Europe

Eastern Europe is a diverse geographical area that has achieved some political unity since World War II as the result of its over-all acceptance of Communism as its guiding political philosophy. Although Eastern Europe is divided into a number of sovereign states, the policies of the Soviet Union are paramount in almost all of them and must be considered by them in every important decision.

Before World War II, several European powers had contended for control of Eastern Europe. Germany attempted to dominate it commercially and then politically; France built up a system of alliances within the area by which it hoped to counter the intentions of Germany; the Soviet Union had hopes of influencing the policies of the East European governments, but achieved very little success in the interwar years. After 1945, a new balance was created, characterized by:

1) Soviet acquisitions of territory during the period from 1939 to 1945. These included the annexation of Estonia, Latvia, and Lithuania and the incorporation of about one-third of the former Polish territory, a part of former German East Prussia, the Ruthenian region of Czechoslovakia, and the province of Bessarabia and part of Bukovina, taken from Romania, as well as parts of Finland.

2) Postwar Soviet domination of the East European states, the establishment there of Soviet garrisons, and the imposition of Communist governments by illegal or quasi-legal means. The last Communist government to be established was that of Czechoslovakia, in February, 1948. Later in the same year, the first significant breach in the Soviet control of Eastern Europe occurred when Tito was denounced by the Cominform for his ideological deviations from the Moscow line and economic aid was withheld from Yugoslavia. The basic reason was that the Yugoslav Communist Party had won power without Russian assistance and was regarded as unreliable. Soon afterward, Yugoslavia was expelled from the Cominform. There have since been attempts to heal the breach, but none of them has achieved more than partial success. But they did cause Albania, which had broken away from Yugoslav tutelage and purged its own Titoists after Yugoslavia's expulsion from the Cominform, to shift its allegiance from Moscow to Peking.

3) The association of each of these countries (except Yugoslavia and Albania) in the military and political organization known as the

Line shading indicates areas annexed by the U.S.S.R. from 1939 to 1945

Warsaw Pact and in the Council for Mutual Economic Assistance. The purpose of these organizations is to coordinate political as well as military and economic policies within the bloc.

34. Languages and Peoples of Eastern Europe*

Eastern Europe is often regarded—though not entirely correctly—as a group of lands inhabited primarily by Slavs. The Slavs are those peoples who speak one of the Slavic languages. These include Russian, the West Slavic group including Polish and Czech, and the South Slavic tongues such as Serbo-Croat and Bulgarian. It is commonly held that the Slavs originated in what is today Poland and that they—or at least their language and culture—spread slowly southward into the Balkan Peninsula and eastward into Russia. The geographical unity of the Slavic settlement was first breached by the arrival of non-Slavs, especially the Magyars (Hungarians), Romanians, and Germans. This division was then aggravated by the cultural differences that gradually emerged among the Slavs themselves.

The ancestors of the Hungarians came into the area about the year 900 (although in part they are probably also descended from Attila's Huns, who made their headquarters on the Danube in the fifth century) and settled in the Plain of Hungary. The Romanians derived from the Romanized peoples of the Balkan Peninsula, who at one time must have spoken Latin. How these groups came to be concentrated largely in modern Romania is not clearly understood. Germans began to move into the area from the west during the Middle Ages, and they formed many compact colonies, most of which have been uprooted and driven back to Germany since World War II.

In time, most of the Slav peoples were converted to Christianity—those in the south and southeast mainly by missionaries from Constantinople, those in the remainder of the territory by missionaries from Rome. This is reflected today in their affiliation with either the Orthodox or the Roman church and even in the alphabets adopted. In Serbia (eastern Yugoslavia), Bulgaria, and the Soviet Union the Cyrillic script, derived from classical Greek by Greek missionaries, is still used. This script has disappeared from Romania only in comparatively recent times.

There is a common feeling, to a degree, throughout the Slavic world of Eastern Europe. Most Slavs—the Poles are a notable exception—tend to think of themselves as one people, but the differences among them go deeper than the small contrasts in language would suggest. At present, a façade of unity has been imposed on

* See Map 11 for explanation of major language families.

Eastern Europe by the Soviet Union, and, temporarily at least, it covers the smoldering frictions and feuds of the peoples and countries of Eastern Europe. Some of these, such as that between Serb and Bulgar, are allowed to come into the open. Others such as that between the Poles and Czechs might come to the surface if Soviet supervision and control were relaxed.

71

35. East European Refugees

In the course of the last thousand years, settlers from Central Europe have been gradually penetrating the Slavic lands of Eastern Europe. This was the "frontier" of Medieval Europe, thinly populated and underdeveloped, into which the Germans expanded. Slavs were either forced farther east or Germanized. From the days of the Roman Empire, Italians, too, were in the Balkans, especially in Dalmatia, once the site of the imperial capital.

In 1919–20, boundaries were redrawn in Eastern Europe to correspond to a considerable extent with the linguistic divisions. Nevertheless, significant German-speaking minorities remained in almost all East European countries, and Italian-speaking groups remained in Yugoslavia, Hungarians in Slovakia and Romania, Bulgarians in Romania and Greece, Albanians and Turks in Greece, and Ukrainians in Poland, Czechoslovakia, and Romania. By 1945, many of these minority groups had either fled or been expelled. Some, such as the Baltic Germans living in those Baltic states that were annexed by the Soviet Union in 1939, had left their East European homes during World War II.

The exact number of refugees since 1944 will never be known, but it is probably at least about 12 million. The largest group, about six million, came from the lands east of the Oder and Neisse that had passed under Polish rule; the next largest consisted of the so-called Sudeten Germans of western Czechoslovakia. Other groups came from eastern Czechoslovakia, Romania, Greece, Albania, Bulgaria, and Yugoslavia.

This population shift created problems not only in the countries from which they fled or were expelled but also in West Germany, where the majority settled. The former countries suffered from a shortage of skilled labor; West Germany, temporarily at least, suffered from overcrowding. By now, however, the refugees have been largely absorbed by the West German economy, and the problem they pose today is more political than economic, because the refugee organizations are pushing for the recovery of Germany's lost lands to the east.

The flight of the Germans westward was not the only large-scale migration of the years following World War II. The Italians left the Yugoslav coastlands, which they had inhabited since the Middle Ages, and many Poles were resettled from the Soviet Union to the western areas of Poland that were made vacant by the expulsion

Estimated Number of
REFUGEES

6,000,000
4,000,000
2,000,000
1,000,000
500,000

GERMANS
OTHERS

FINLAND — Karelia

Baltic States

U.S.S.R.

Belorussia

WESTERN EUROPE

EAST GERMANY

POLAND

Ukraine

CZECHOSLOVAKIA

1956

HUNGARY

ROMANIA

YUGOSLAVIA

BULGARIA

ITALY

ALBANIA

Greece

Turkey

0   100   200   300 miles

of the Germans. Turks were driven out of Bulgaria, and (on a very small scale) Czechoslovakia and Hungary exchanged each other's Hungarian and Czechoslovak minorities. Large numbers of Slavs and Albanians were driven from Greece, and many Greeks and Italians from Albania.

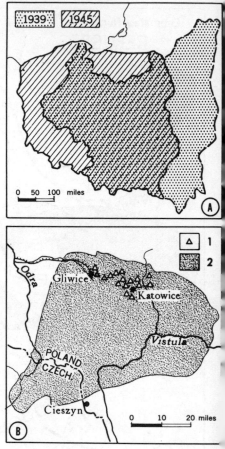

A. *Boundaries in 1939 and 1945*
B. *Upper Silesia industrial area:* 1—iron and steel plant; 2—coal basin
C. *Mineral resources and industry:* 1—coal deposits; 2—lignite deposits; 3—petroleum fields; 4—major industrial area

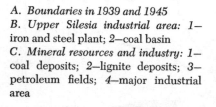

36. Poland

The state of Poland emerged just a thousand years ago, its geographical center in the plains between Warsaw and Poznań. It expanded westward to the valley of the Oder and eastward into Russia. In time, Germans encroached on western Poland, but Poland continued, until the seventeenth century, to expand eastward, merging with Lithuania and temporarily occupying some Russian cities, among them Kiev.

However, internal weaknesses led to the loss of territory and brought about the three partitions of Poland (1772–96), during which Poland disappeared from the map. A small Polish state, known as the Grand Duchy of Warsaw, was re-established by Na-

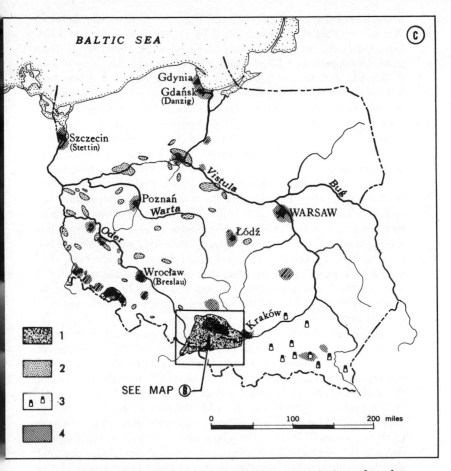

BALTIC SEA

Szczecin
(Stettin)

Gdynia
Gdańsk
(Danzig)

Poznań
Warta

Vistula

Bug

WARSAW

Łódź

Oder

Wrocław
(Breslau)

Kraków

1
2
3
4

SEE MAP Ⓑ

0   100   200 miles

poleon, but it was acquired by Czarist Russia in 1815. At first this Polish state was autonomous, but after the unsuccessful revolution of 1830, it was made an administrative part of Russia. And the last independent Polish territory, the tiny Republic of Cracow, was annexed by Austria in 1848, because it had served as a center for Polish nationalism.

Modern Poland was created in 1918. At the Paris Conference, an attempt was made to adjust its boundaries to correspond with the area of the Polish language. Thus, East Prussia was cut off from the rest of Germany, and the Upper Silesian industrial region was partitioned between Germany and Poland. Poland was left to establish her own boundary in the east. This she did in the course of a short and successful war (1919–20), and the eastern boundary between Russia and Poland was established by the Treaty of Riga in 1921. Included in the area that Poland acquired were many White Russians, Ukrainians, and Lithuanians who never became reconciled to Polish rule. Poland also seized Vilna from Lithuania, but was herself the victim of aggression by Czechoslovakia, which occupied the predominantly Polish Teschen area while Poland was preoccupied with her war with Russia. Poland recovered Teschen under the Munich agreement but returned part of it to Czechoslovakia at the end of World War II. In September, 1939, Poland was invaded by Germany, and the Russians, by agreement with Hitler, reoccupied the eastern third of the country, which, with slight boundary modifications, they still retain. During the war, it was proposed that Poland be allowed to make up this loss by annexing the German territory lying east of the Oder and the Neisse rivers. To this area has also been added the port of Stettin (Szczecin), which lies on the west bank of the Oder. This transfer of territory has not been confirmed by a peace treaty and has not, in fact, been formally recognized by the Western powers. But it seems unlikely to be reversed, in view of the expulsion of the German population and the resettlement of this area by Poles.

The modern Polish state is a compact area of 120,359 square miles, with a population of 29,965,000. The territorial changes of the war years, involving a westward shift of Poland's geographical center, have actually increased its resources, although the area of the state is considerably smaller than it was before World War II.

The western territories occupied by Poland in 1945 had formerly been inhabited by about 8.9 million people, not more than 1 million of them ethnically Polish. The Germans either fled or were driven out, and the territories have been occupied by Poles. Today the total population of these areas is close to that of the prewar period, and in some sections exceeds it.

Poland is largely an agricultural country, although its manufacturing industries are rapidly growing in importance. In fact, the number of people employed in manufacturing has recently exceeded that in agriculture. As a result of recent boundary changes, Poland now contains all of the Upper Silesian coal field and industrial region, as well as the small but important coal field of Lower Silesia. In continental Europe, Poland is second only to West Germany in coal production. She also produces lead, zinc, and some other nonferrous metals, as well as a small quantity of petroleum.

Poland's manufacturing industries have been greatly expanded since the end of World War II—especially the iron and steel industries, which now produce over 7 million tons of steel a year. Much of this new industrial capacity was acquired by the annexation of the German industrial area of Silesia, and serves as the basis for further subsequent expansion. The chemical and fertilizer, automobile, ship-building, and engineering industries have also grown considerably.

Poland now has a coastline of about 200 miles, with important and well-equipped ports at Danzig, Gdynia, and Stettin. The industrial growth and commerce of Poland are dependent to a large extent on her Communist neighbors, but an important foreign trade is carried on with the free world, especially the export of coal and the products of many of Poland's engineering industries.

Agriculture, however, is lagging. It is organized mainly in small peasant farms, on which traditional methods of cultivation are still used. Attempts to collectivize have broken down in the face of the resistance of the peasants, and most of the agricultural land is still in the hands of the peasants.

A Communist government assumed power in Poland in 1944, but until 1947 it contained representatives of one faction of those non-Communist Poles who had escaped to the West after 1939; another group, however, continued to maintain a government-in-exile in London. Thereafter, Poland was completely under Soviet domination until 1956, when economic austerity and disillusionment with Soviet policy led to riots. The government made concessions and held off a renewed attempt, including a personal visit by Khrushchev, to reimpose a tight Soviet control. Wladyslaw Gomulka, who had been expelled from both his office and the Party during the Stalinist period, was rehabilitated and became First Secretary of the Polish United Workers' (Communist) Party and the most important figure in the country.

Poland remains a Communist state, but it has not blindly followed the Soviet line. In many ways, the austerities have been eased and restrictions on personal freedom reduced. Poland is today one of the freest and most Western-oriented of the members of the Soviet bloc.

37. Czechoslovakia

The land of the Czechs and the Slovaks was created in 1918 when the former Austro-Hungarian Empire broke up. Czechs and Slovaks were culturally related, and their languages were similar. Each seemed too small numerically to exist as a separate state, so they joined voluntarily to form Czechoslovakia.

Czechoslovakia was the only East European state to make a success of democratic government. Nevertheless, it faced acute internal problems. For one thing, a balance between the Czechs and the Slovaks did not exist. Not only were the Czechs more numerous, but they were more advanced technically, better educated, and politically more mature; moreover, they controlled much of the country's industry and dominated the civil service.

Living beside the Czechs and the Slovaks were German, Polish, and Hungarian minorities, together making up about 4 million out of a total population of only about 13.6 million. Of these, the so-called Sudeten Germans numbered more than 3 million and were by far the most politically important. To a large extent, the minorities lived near the country's borders in compact areas, where they formed the majority of the population. The minority problem became crucial with the rise of Nazism and in 1938–39 served as the instrument for Hitler's destruction of the country.

The Czechoslovak state was restored in 1945, minus part of Teschen and the small territory of Carpatho-Ruthenia in the east (*see Map 33*), which was inhabited by people related to the Ukrainians and which had been ceded to the U.S.S.R. (A large number of Jews, who before the war had formed the most important single ethnic group in the Carpatho-Ruthenian population, had been killed or expelled during the war.) Most of the German minority has been expelled from Czechoslovakia (*see Map 35*). Czechoslovakia was already an important industrial country before World War II, and its industrial plant was greatly expanded during the German occupation. It increased still further after 1945. In particular, much new industry has been established in Slovakia in an attempt to raise the standard of living in this previously underdeveloped region of the country.

Agriculture in Czechoslovakia, unlike that of Poland, has largely been collectivized and mechanized, and the new buildings of the collective farms are conspicuous features of the landscape today.

Czechoslovakia has been a docile member of the Communist

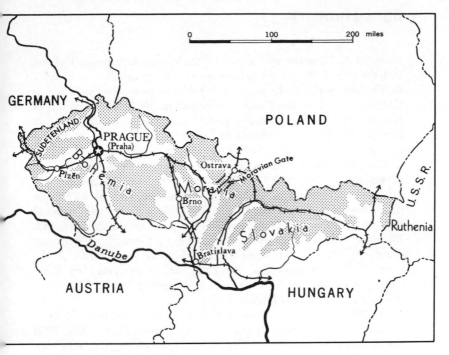

Highland areas are stippled

bloc, and its Communist leaders—headed by Antonin Novotny, the President and First Secretary of the Party—have in all respects followed the Moscow line. There has been less unrest in Czechoslovakia than in some other Communist countries, partly because the Communist Party was initially stronger, polling 38 per cent of the vote in the first postwar elections, and partly because material standards were rather higher than in other Communist countries. Nevertheless, the workers of the major Czech industrial cities revolted in 1953, in many cases under the leadership of the Communist factory militia themselves. And the internal history of the Communist regime has been characterized by exceptionally severe purges in the leadership, in which open anti-Semitism has played a prominent part. Czechoslovakia's strong pan-Slav tradition has been reinforced by fear of a revived Germany, which has intensified the country's dependence on the Soviet Union.

38. Hungary

Until 1918, Hungary was a part of the Austro-Hungarian Empire, and the proud Hungarian people ruled a large number of Slovaks, Romanians, Serbs, and Croats, who together numbered as many as themselves. When the Empire collapsed in 1918, the kingdom of Hungary was more drastically partitioned than any other state in Europe. Its area was reduced to less than one-third of its former size, and it lost more than half of its former population.

The Hungarians took their losses extremely hard, and it is no exaggeration to say that for the next twenty years the country was in a sort of national mourning; the single objective of its foreign policy was to make alliances that would allow it to regain some of the lost territory. This was the reason for Hungary's association with Mussolini and her later alliance with Hitler's Germany. Before and during World War II, some territorial gains were made at the expense of Czechoslovakia, Romania, and Yugoslavia, but these were lost in 1945 when the boundaries existing before 1937 were restored in Central and Eastern Europe.

In 1944–45, the Soviet armies overran Hungary and set up a Communist government favorable to the Soviet Union. The 1956 uprising, an attempt to establish a more liberal regime, was suppressed by Soviet forces. For a period of some five years, Hungary, under its Prime Minister, Janos Kadar, was under strict Soviet control. Since 1961, however, these restrictions have begun to be relaxed, and a degree of liberalism is beginning to appear which may eventually match that of Poland.

Hungary is largely an agricultural country, but manufacturing and, to a lesser extent, mining have long played an important role in its economy. Like other Communist countries, however, it is collectivizing its agriculture and building up its manufacturing industries. Prominent among these is the Sztalinvaros steel works, built on the Danube below Budapest and supplied in part with materials brought by barge on the Danube from the Soviet Union. Electrical, radio, and electronic industries, among others, have been expanded and now supply many other members of the Communist bloc.

Hungary is one of the few East European countries that does not have any significant area dominated by minority groups, although the population includes large numbers of persons of German, Jewish, and Slavic origin—a result of the ethnic dispersion that took

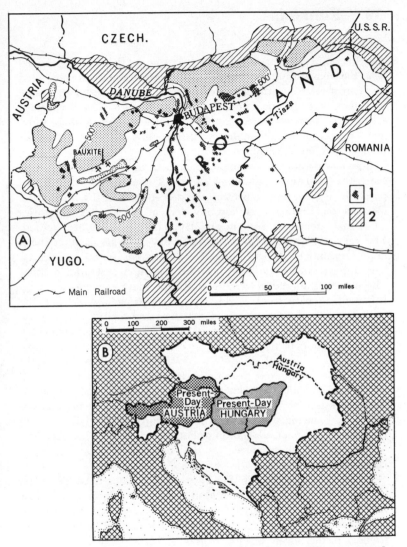

A. *Present-day Hungary:* 1—vineyards; 2—Hungarian peoples in surrounding countries. Highlands are stippled

B. *Austria-Hungary* (at the time of World War I)

place in the Austro-Hungarian Empire. Its boundaries were trimmed so drastically in 1919–20 that only predominantly Hungarian territory was left.

39. Romania

The Republic of Romania suggests by its name that it is descended from the Roman Empire. Much of its territory was indeed conquered by Roman armies in the second century A.D. and, under the name of Dacia, was absorbed into the Roman Empire. The Romanians claim to be descended from the Roman settlers of this remote province of the Empire, although not all scholars and few of Romania's neighbors accept the claim.

Romania is compact in shape but broken up by ranges of mountains—the Carpathian Mountains and the Transylvanian Alps. It was probably in these mountains that the descendants of the Romanized Dacians found refuge from later invaders, and it was here, centuries later, that groups of German and Hungarian peoples also settled. The various parts of modern Romania have at various times been under Byzantine, Polish-Lithuanian, Hungarian, Turkish, Russian, Serbian, and Austrian rule, or have been independent principalities. The present state did not emerge until the mid-nineteenth century. It benefited greatly from World War I, an outcome of which was the near doubling of Romania's area. At the same time, the newly expanded boundaries, which brought most of the Romanian people within the limits of the state, also encompassed Hungarians, Serbs, Bulgars, Ukrainians, Russians, Germans, Jews, and even Turks. In 1918, Romania annexed Bessarabia, inhabited by mixed, predominantly non-Romanian peoples. In 1940, the Soviet Union demanded the retrocession of Bessarabia and the cession of Bukovina and obtained it. Romania was also forced to return southern Dobruja to Bulgaria by the joint arbitration of Hitler and Stalin. These cessions were confirmed in the peace treaties, but that of Transylvania to Hungary was not.

Romania entered World War II in 1941 as the ally of Germany, but she played only a minor role in the Russian campaign. In August, 1944, when Germany's defeat seemed imminent, a *coup d'état* overthrew the pro-German government and established one more friendly to the Soviet Union. In March, 1945, a Communist-dominated government took office, and in 1947, the democratic opposition parties were completely suppressed and King Michael forced to abdicate. Gheorghiu-Dej became Premier in 1952 and later became Chairman of the State Council and Secretary of the Communist Party. He is without dispute the strongest man in Romania.

Romania is a country rich in agricultural and mineral resources.

82

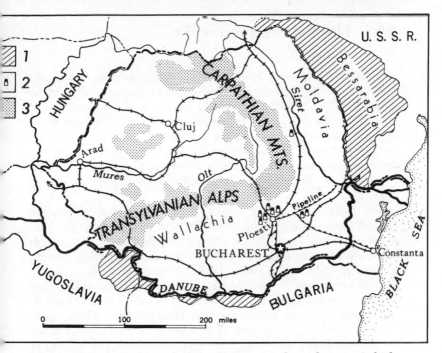

1—Romanian peoples beyond the borders; 2—petroleum deposits; 3—highland areas

While before the war the country had little industry, its rate of industrial growth in recent years has been the highest in the Communist bloc. This has caused tension between Romania and the Soviet Union, since Romania has been developing industries that should, according to Moscow's plans, have been left to other members of the bloc. The chief mineral resource of Romania is petroleum, but even now it accounts for little more than 1 per cent of the world's production.

The present population of 18,567,000 is made up largely of Romanians—about 86 per cent. Hungarian-speaking people constitute about 9 per cent, and Germans about 2 per cent. These two groups are found mainly in the upland basin of Transylvania, in the heart of the country where their ancestors settled during the Middle Ages. Ukrainians, Serbs, Turks, Greeks, and Tartars make up smaller communities within the Romanian nation. Despite mass slaughter by the Nazis and the native Iron Guard fascists, and Romania's traditional intense anti-Semitism, Jews still form over 1 per cent of the population.

40.   The Balkan Peninsula

"Balkan" has become a byword for political instability and chaos. This springs both from the ethnic confusion of the area and from the long period of Turkish rule, which, for much of the area, ended only in the last half of the nineteenth century and, for some areas as late as the early years of the twentieth. Turkish rule was extremely oppressive. It allowed neither economic development nor the emergence of local political institutions. The area of Turkish conquest and rule remains economically backward and politically immature.

The Balkans are a very mountainous region. In the west, the Dinaric system extends south from the Alps through Yugoslav Dalmatia into Albania and Greece. Farther east, the Rhodope Mountains run south from the east-west Balkan range proper, cutting through western Bulgaria and Greek Thrace. Between them is a trough, drained northward by the Morava River and southward by the Vardar. Near Niš (Nish), in Yugoslavia, it is joined by another valley, through part of which runs the Maritsa River, which opens southeastward in the direction of Istanbul (Constantinople). Along the Danube Valley and these two valley routes have passed most of the numerous invaders of the Balkans, and through them now run the chief railroads and roads of the peninsula. The mountains that lie between these valleys have hindered communications, but they have also provided for the natives regions of refuge from invaders.

The more westerly range, the Dinaric Alps, are broad and rugged and cut off most of the Balkan Peninsula from the Adriatic Sea. The two easiest natural routes across them are in the extreme northwest (behind the ports of Trieste and Rijeka) and across Albania. The former is much used today; it has roads and railroads and is an outlet to the sea for the commerce of northern Yugoslavia and of much of the middle Danube Basin. The route across Albania, where the River Drin has cut a passage through the mountains, was most recently used by Mussolini in his invasion of Greece during World War II. The Greek port of Salonika provides an outlet to the sea for the central region of the Vardar and Morava valleys.

The route pattern of the Balkan Peninsula is remarkably simple and is fixed by the lines of the main rivers. These trace not only the former invasion routes but also the present highways of commerce.

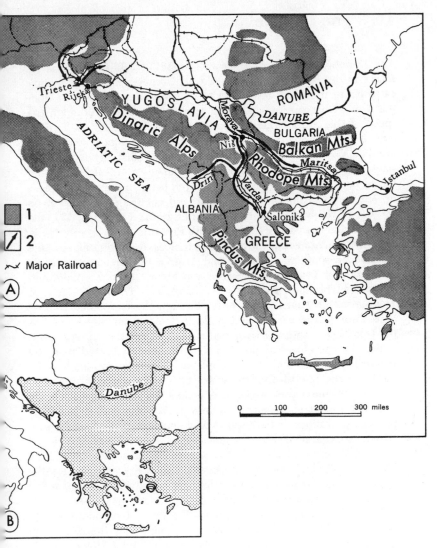

A. *Present-day Balkan nations:* 1—highland area; 2—main route through
highland areas
B. *Extent of Ottoman Empire in Europe, 1815*

41. The Danube

The Danube, the longest river in Europe (1,770 miles), has its source in the Black Forest of southwest Germany and flows mainly eastward to the Black Sea. Most of its tributaries flow into it from the Alps. It becomes navigable in southern Germany, although the speed of the current there sometimes makes upstream traffic difficult. It flows through Austria, Czechoslovakia, Hungary, and northern Yugoslavia and then forms the boundary first between Yugoslavia and Romania and then between Romania and Bulgaria. In the lowest part of its course, it makes a large bend to the north, breaks up into the distributaries of its delta, and enters the Black Sea. As a result of the Soviet annexation of Bessarabia (*see Map 33*), the Soviet Union now shares the delta with Romania.

There are numerous physical hindrances to navigation on the Danube. In southern Germany and Austria, the stream is swift; in Hungary and Yugoslavia, the river spreads out over the plain, and its channel becomes shallow and changeable. On the borders of Yugoslavia and Romania, it passes through the Carpathian Mountains through the narrow and difficult defile commonly known as the Iron Gate; there the river bed is rugged and the current swift.

But the usefulness of the Danube has been restricted more by political influences than by geographical ones. It lay too long on the border of the Turkish Empire, where conditions were too disturbed for it to become a great highway of commerce. Attempts were made during the nineteenth century to improve both the political and the physical conditions. Freedom of navigation was assured, and an international commission was established. This has since functioned irregularly, and now there are two such commissions—one for the lower river (which the Soviet Union belongs to) and one for the upper. But real improvements will come only with a more unified control of the rivers of the Danube basin.

In recent years, the association of the Danubian countries with Germany brought about a revival of shipping. Now the river is an important avenue of commerce between the Soviet Union and its Danubian satellites upstream as far as Bratislava, Czechoslovakia. This is the point near which the Danube crosses from Central Europe into Communist Eastern Europe. It is also important in the trade of Austria and Yugoslavia with the Soviet bloc and West Germany.

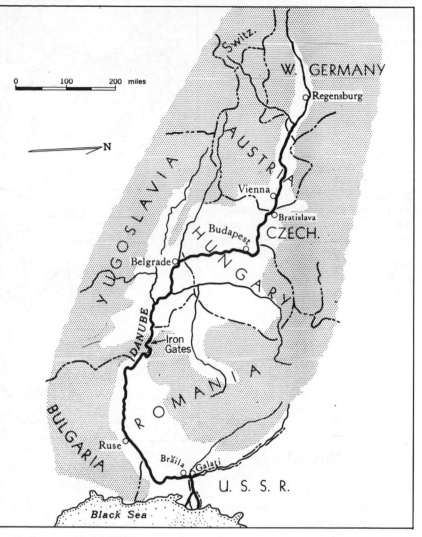

Highland areas are stippled

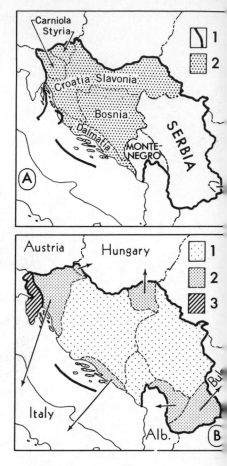

A. After World War I (1919): 1—
boundary of newly created Yugoslavia;
2—sections of former Austria-Hungary
ceded to Yugoslavia

B. During World War II: 1—puppet
states; *2*—territories directly administered or annexed by Italy, Bulgaria,
Albania, and Hungary, as shown by
arrows; *3*—annexed by Yugoslavia,
1947

*C. Present-day provinces and major
cities*

42. Yugoslavia

Yugoslavia was created after World War I by the grouping of a
number of southern Slav peoples around the old kingdom of Serbia.
The union of these peoples was far from harmonious, and the new
state was beset by serious internal and external problems.

As was so often the case in Eastern Europe after World War I,
it proved to be difficult to draw a boundary between the Slav
peoples and their neighbors. In the northwest, there were groups of
Yugoslavs (Slovenes) within the German-speaking country of Austria. Along the northern boundary, Yugoslavs (Croats and Serbs)

lived alongside Hungarians and Romanians. There were large numbers of Germans and smaller numbers of Hungarians in parts of Yugoslavia, especially Slovenia, Croatia, and the Voivodina. In the east, trouble threatened from the ancient rivalry of Serbs and Bulgars. In the south, Serbs, Bulgars, Albanians, and even occasional Greeks lived intermingled. The picture was so complicated by ancient claims to territory and by the confused ethnic pattern of the twentieth century that no boundary could possibly satisfy the hopes of all. Finally, along the Adriatic coast, there had long been Italian settlements, which provided the basis for an Italian claim to the area.

This ethnic picture was further complicated by the economic one.

89

The interior of Yugoslavia was cut off from the Adriatic Sea by the rugged Dinaric Alps across which commerce was difficult and in many areas impossible. Only the ports of Trieste and Rijeka (Fiume) commanded good routes through the mountains and into the interior. Yugoslavia failed to get permanent possession of these ports after World War I, but after 1945 she was able to incorporate Rijeka into her territory (see Map 43). To the south, the Yugoslavs were dependent on their transit rights to the Greek port of Salonika, where they had a small free-port area (see Map 43).

Relations between Yugoslavia and its neighbors Albania and Bulgaria have been strained. Before the war, Yugoslav-Bulgar relations were poisoned by the Macedonian question; since 1945, they have reflected the relations between Belgrade and Moscow. Both before and since the war, relations between Yugoslavia and Albania have been characterized by Yugoslav efforts to secure a dominant role in Albanian political life and Albanian alternation between acceptance of Yugoslav influence and resistance to it.

Yugoslavia—the name means "Land of the Southern Slavs"—covers a wider variety of peoples than Czechoslovakia. The two largest groups in the population are the Serbs and the Croats. In effect, they speak the same language, but they write it according to different scripts. Furthermore, in religion the Serbs are generally Eastern Orthodox and the Croats Roman Catholic. Between the two World Wars, the chief internal division was that between these two peoples—the Serbs with their long tradition of revolt against the Turks, and the Croats, who have inherited much of the culture of the Austrians and Hungarians, under whose rule they once lived.

The Slovenes are a Slav people living in the extreme northwest. They are a smaller and more Westernized group. On the other side, in the extreme southeast, the Macedonians are much less developed. Their language resembles Serbo-Croat, but it has been claimed by both Bulgars and Serbs as a branch of their language. In Bosnia, Moslems form a majority of the population, and form a link between Yugoslavia and the Middle East. And the Montenegrins although not a numerous group, are proud of their heritage of resistance to foreign rule through the centuries, when the rest of the country was under Turkish, Hungarian, and Austrian domination.

At first, the Serbs attempted to control the country; they were resisted, especially by the Croats, and a kind of federal structure was introduced in 1939. The present constitution is federal, and the province boundaries are drawn to correspond as closely as possible to the boundaries of the ethnic groups. To some extent, the problem was simplified by the departure of many of the Italians and the expulsion of part of the German minority. In the federal system today, there are six provinces (Slovenia, Croatia, Serbia, Bosnia, Herzegovina, and Macedonia) and two special areas—the Vojvodina and the so-called Kosmet (Kossovo-Metohija), in each of which the population is extremely mixed.

The internal divisions were an important factor in Yugoslavia's weakness before World War II, and they contributed to the German invasion of the country in April, 1941. Although the country was overrun by German (assisted by Italian) forces, the rugged terrain made close control impossible. Resistance groups—both Serb and Croat, pro-Western and Communist—began to operate. There was a very confused period when it was not clear whether the resistance groups, or Partisans, were devoting more energy to fighting one another or their common enemy. From this confusion, the Communist Partisans, led by Josip Broz (Tito) came to the fore and at the end of the war took over the government of the country.

The Communist government of Yugoslavia modeled its federal constitution on the Soviet and for a time acted in close liaison with the Kremlin. In 1948, friction developed (*see Map 33*); Yugoslavia resisted Soviet attempts to dominate and control its economic development in the interests of the Soviet Union, and consequently was expelled from the Cominform. It has remained a Communist nation, but in most respects has been independent of the Soviet bloc—and in some matters has sided with the West. Yugoslav relations with the Soviet Union have fluctuated and at times have been strongly hostile. At present, however, they are warmer than at any time since the development of the breach in 1948. Khrushchev has been welcomed in Belgrade, and it is reported that Yugoslavia may even join the Communist Council for Mutual Economic Assistance (*see Map 33*). In 1963, a new constitution was introduced, which, among other things, increases the role assigned to Parliament.

43. Trieste and Macedonia

The ports of Trieste and Rijeka (Fiume) are the best points of entry to all of northern Yugoslavia for seaborne commerce. Under the Austro-Hungarian Empire, they were inhabited by mixed populations in which no single ethnic group was predominant, although their hinterlands were largely Slavic. The new Yugoslav state gained possession of Fiume, but it was seized shortly afterward (September, 1919) by a band of Italian freebooters led by the novelist and Italian nationalist Gabriele D'Annunzio. However, the Italian Government did not fully support him and acquiesced in the establishment of the Free City of Fiume. In 1924, Mussolini reached an agreement with the Yugoslav Government whereby Fiume was incorporated into Italy, and the Yugoslavs were left to make the best they could of the port of Fiume's suburb, Susak. In both Trieste and Fiume, as well as in other parts of the area known as Venezia Giulia, Mussolini pursued a policy of colonization and forced Italianization, going so far as to destroy tombstones with Slavic inscriptions. After World War II, Yugoslavia again got possession of Rijeka and claimed also the port and hinterland of Trieste. This area was occupied by Allied troops and became for a time free territory. After repeated failures by Italy and Yugoslavia to agree on the future of the territory as a whole, it was divided between them in 1954. Trieste and its immediate hinterland, the former so-called Zone A, were included in Italy; the rest, the former Zone B, was incorporated into Yugoslavia. Trieste continues to serve as a port for Yugoslavia, but the Yugoslavs are improving the port of Rijeka, whose volume of commerce is increasing. In fact, Rijeka is now by far Yugoslavia's most important port.

"Macedonia" has almost become a synonym for "ethnic confusion." It constitutes a sort of meeting place of Serbs, Bulgars, Greeks, Albanians, and Romanians, and has been claimed by all of them and has been fought for repeatedly. The problem is complicated by the fact that across Macedonia lies the Vardar valley route to the Aegean Sea, and on its southern border is the important port of Salonika (Thessalonike). This valley has, since classical times, been the most important route from the Mediterranean Sea into the Balkan Peninsula.

Most of Macedonia is now divided between Yugoslavia and Greece. In the Greek part, which together with Greek Thrace forms the Government-General of Northern Greece, the general policy is one of Hellenization. Yugoslav Macedonia, which seethed with re-

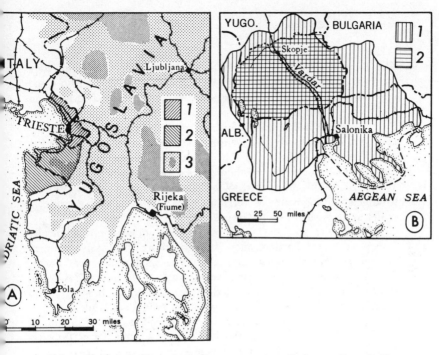

A. *Trieste: 1*—former Zone A, Italian occupation; *2*—former Zone B, Yugoslav occupation; *3*—highlands
B. *Macedonia: 1*—approximate cultural area of Macedonia; *2*—Yugoslav province of Macedonia

bellion prior to 1939, is now organized as a province in a federal state. The use of the Macedonian language, very closely related to Serb, is encouraged by the government. The Macedonian university in the city of Skoplje has done everything possible to stimulate the use of Macedonian as a literary language. (Skoplje was devastated by an earthquake in July, 1963, but present reports are that it will be rebuilt.)

44. Bulgaria

The Bulgars are regarded as a South Slav people, although they derive their name from invaders from the Asiatic steppe who came into this area and settled in the seventh century A.D. The state, in fact, was created by Slav peasants under Bulgar leadership. The Bulgarian state had a stormy history until it succumbed to Turkish invasions in the fourteenth century. Under Russian sponsorship it reappeared as a state in the last quarter of the nineteenth century, but inherited the ancient feuds of the Balkan peoples. In the Balkan Wars (1912–13) and World War I, Bulgaria lost southern Dobruja to Romania, fragments of territory to Yugoslavia, and its former outlet to the Aegean Sea to Greece.

Bulgaria was stripped of all territories that were not ethnically Bulgarian, and it became, like Hungary, a small, cohesive country with no significant minority groups except a small number of "Turks" (largely descendants of Bulgarian converts to Islam) and Greeks, most of whom have been expelled. Bulgaria was left, however, with a feeling of bitter resentment toward its neighbors, and its policy seems even today to be colored by this as well as by its Communist ideology. Between the two World Wars, the demands of Bulgaria for territorial revision kept the Balkan Peninsula in a turmoil.

As a result of the joint arbitration of Hitler and Stalin, Bulgaria recovered the overwhelmingly Bulgarian southern Dobruja from Romania in September, 1940. This was one of the few territorial transfers of the World War II period that were not reversed after the war was over.

Bulgaria is one of the most predominantly agricultural countries in Europe. It has a strong tradition of equalitarian peasant democracy, which was largely responsible for the fact that, alone in the Balkans, Bulgaria saved its entire Jewish population during the war. This tradition and the absence of large landholders or capitalists produced a vigorous resistance to the seizure of power by the Communists, which the latter were able to crush only by the large-scale use of terror. Recent attempts to build up modern industry have not been particularly successful, and Bulgaria is poorly endowed with fuel and mineral resources. Also, her climate is too dry for hydroelectric power of any importance.

Bulgaria has been an obedient member of the Communist bloc and has done her utmost to embarrass her pro-Western neighbors, Turkey and Greece. Since the death of Georgi Dimitrov and the

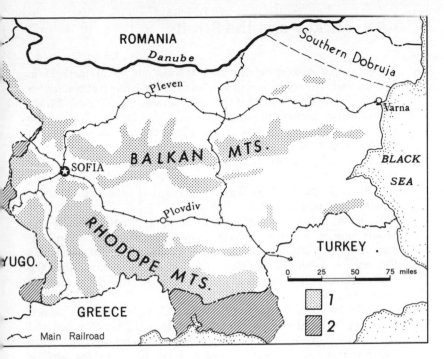

1—highlands; *2*—territory lost 1913–19

execution of Traicho Kostov, most of her leaders have been political nonentities who can be relied upon to follow the Moscow line. At present, the First Secretary of the Party and Communist leader is Todor Zhivkov. Periodically, Bulgaria revives her old claim to Yugoslav Macedonia, but this is always in line with the current Soviet policy toward Yugoslavia.

95

45. Turkey and the Straits

Turkey is an Asiatic country that retains one small foothold in Europe and, consequently, has control over the important waterways that link the Black Sea with the Aegean Sea. The Turkish Straits consist of two narrow, twisting waterways—the Dardanelles and the Bosporus—linked by the Sea of Marmara. At their narrowest, both Straits are less than a mile wide and can easily be commanded by the Turks. The Turkish Sultans had formerly "closed" the Straits—that is, they fortified the shores and exercised the right to deny passage through them to non-Turkish vessels, but conceded the right of nonbelligerents to use them.

In 1915, a British army tried to force a passage through the Straits in order to bring aid to the hard-pressed armies of the Russian Czar. The attack on the Gallipoli Peninsula, which commands the entrance to the Dardanelles, was a disastrous failure. After the war was over, the British and their allies were strongly in favor of "open" Straits.

By the Treaty of Lausanne (1923), which ended Turkey's participation in World War I, the Straits were declared demilitarized and open to all shipping. The Western Allies who negotiated the treaty could at that time foresee the need to send their warships into the Black Sea against the Soviet Union. In 1935, Turkey appealed for a revision of the Treaty of Lausanne. By the Treaty of Montreux (1936), it was agreed that Turkey should again be allowed to fortify the Straits and to place restrictions on the passage of warships through the waterways. The Western powers were now anxious to place some barrier in the way of the egress of the Soviet fleet into the Mediterranean Sea. Standing on these rights, Turkey denied passage through the Straits to Soviet warships in 1945.

The Soviet Union has pressed for some share in garrisoning and guarding the Straits, claiming that they are an essential waterway for her and that, in the hands of other powers, they could be used to threaten the Soviet Union itself. Turkey has refused these demands and has been supported by the Western powers. The Straits continue to be administered under the terms of the Treaty of Montreux.

European Turkey comprises only 3 per cent of the total area of Turkey. It is a region of poor steppe and contributes little to the economic resources of Turkey. On the European shore of the Bosporus, however, is Istanbul (formerly Constantinople). Istanbul was

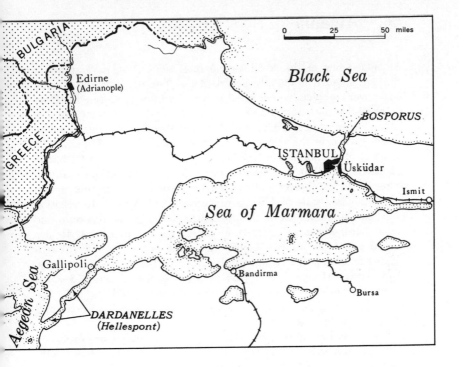

the capital of the Ottoman Empire until 1923, when it was replaced as the seat of government of the Turkish Republic by Ankara, in the heart of Asiatic Turkey. However, Istanbul remains by far the largest city in Turkey and is the terminus of the main trunk railroad of the Balkans, long famous as the route of the Orient Express.

46. Albania

Albania is one of the smallest and most underdeveloped states in Europe. Though nominally a part of the Turkish Empire, Albania was never completely controlled by the Turks, who were effectively deterred by the rugged mountain terrain and the ferocity of the Albanian resistance. There are several dialects of Albanian, a language known in the region before the coming of the Greeks. The majority of the population are Moslem, but there are large Orthodox Christian and Roman Catholic minorities who reflect the cultural influence of the Greeks and the Italians, respectively, in this region.

The modern state of Albania was established in 1912. Its creation satisfied the ambitions of the Albanians, although at the time one could hardly have said that they were ripe for statehood. It also solved a serious problem among the great powers. Serbia (Yugoslavia) and Greece, as well as Italy, all had designs on this territory. And Austria-Hungary was particularly anxious to block Serbian access to the Mediterranean. The easiest course, and the only one on which agreement could be reached, was to give it to none and to make it a separate state.

The boundary drawn for the new state excluded a substantial Albanian minority in Yugoslavia and Greece and included a substantial number of Greeks, who now make up about 2.5 per cent of the population. Hostility with Albania on the one hand and Greece on the other has been a constant feature of the politics of the area. During the 1920's, Yugoslavia and Italy competed for influence over Albania; the Italians gained a large measure of economic and political control over Albania, eventually annexing it and using it as a springboard for the invasion of Greece.

At the close of World War II, the Communist Party, which had conducted a guerrilla war against the Germans and Italians, gained power and then firmly consolidated its position. Albania, in terms of resources and population, is the weakest of the Communist countries of Eastern Europe, but its location on the Mediterranean coast gives it a disproportionate importance and degree of independence from Moscow.

This independence has been demonstrated increasingly in recent years, and, since the Twenty-second CPSU Congress, in the fall of 1961, Albania has quite openly followed the lead of Communist China rather than that of the Soviet Union itself. The reasons for this probably have little to do with the orthodoxy—or any other

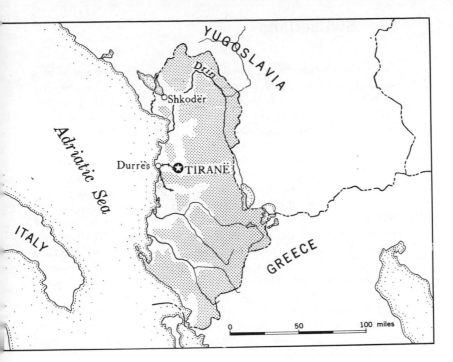

Highland areas are stippled

facet, for that matter—of Communist doctrine in Albania. It is
much more likely that it is connected with the perennial friction in
Albania's relations with Yugoslavia and her fear of Yugoslav domination.

The chief of the Albanian state is Enver Hoxha, the leader of the
"Albanian Army of National Liberation" during World War II. His
policy has been consistently more Albanian than Communist, in so
far as his chief ambition is the territorial aggrandizement of Albania.
It is in line with his policy that he has recently appeared to prefer
the Chinese to the Soviets, with the latter's tendency under Khrushchev to accept "coexistence."

99

47. Switzerland

For over a century, Switzerland has been an island of peace in a war-torn continent. Switzerland is a confederation of twenty-five cantons. When the confederation was first formed in 1291, its federal constitution was made necessary by the physical difficulties of communication and cooperation in the very rugged terrain of the central Alps. It served, however, to attract other small areas to it, and these subsequently became separate cantons in the confederation. The boundaries of the confederation did not reach their present form until 1815, when the last canton, Geneva, was admitted.

The unity and cohesion of Switzerland have been achieved despite serious obstacles. Among these are the divisive influence of the mountains and the division of the people themselves into four separate language groups. Over two-thirds speak German, less than a quarter speak French, and the rest speak Italian and Romansh. All four are now regarded as national or official languages. Each is the predominant language of one or more cantons. A majority of the population (about 56 per cent) are Protestant, and most of the remainder are Roman Catholic. Protestantism tends to predominate in the urban areas, while Catholicism is found primarily in the rural and mountainous areas.

Switzerland was the first state in modern times to declare itself neutral, and this status was guaranteed in 1815 by most of the great powers. Swiss neutrality has since been respected by all.

As an inland and highly industrialized state, Switzerland is dependent upon rights of transit across the territories of all her neighbors. This has presented no problems in peacetime, and Switzerland operates a fleet of Rhine barges from her port of Basel. She also exercises her right of way across France and Italy in order to send goods to their ports for export.

The industries of Switzerland have been adjusted, as it were, to overcome the problems posed by her location. Switzerland has few industrial raw materials, but she does have an abundance of hydroelectric power. She manufactures quality goods for which raw-material and transportation costs are low, but for which the value of labor and skill is high. Dairy farming and tourism are also important in the economy. Her neutrality and stability have also given Switzerland great advantages as a center for banking and international organizations.

One hears little about the government of Switzerland, and its

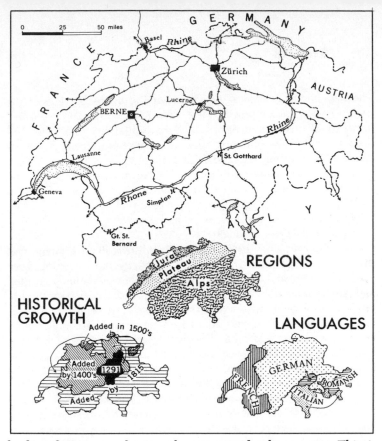

Map labels:
GERMANY

0 25 50 miles

Basel — Rhine
Zürich
FRANCE
Lucerne
BERNE
AUSTRIA
Rhine
Lausanne
St. Gotthard
Geneva — Rhone — Simplon
Gt. St. Bernard
ITALY

REGIONS
Jura
Plateau
Alps

HISTORICAL GROWTH
Added in 1500's
Added by 1400's
1291
by 1815
Added

LANGUAGES
GERMAN
FRENCH
ITALIAN
ROMANSH

leading figures are almost unknown outside the country. This is partly because the country is a confederation and many of the duties of government are carried on at the cantonal level, and partly because the country is a "neutral" and thus has no foreign policy in the accepted sense.

Eight political parties are represented in the Parliament, or National Council, and a majority of its members belong to the Socialist (social democratic) and Radical parties. Switzerland is governed by a collegiate executive, whose members are elected individually by the Federal Council and rotate the Presidency among themselves on an annual basis. By a sort of gentlemen's agreement, all the major democratic parties are represented on the executive roughly in proportion to their strength. The use of the referendum, or direct popular vote, on critical issues tends to take these out of the field of Parliament and party government. Switzerland is the only European country that does not have woman suffrage.

48.   Austria

The Republic of Austria is what remained after the breakup of the Austro-Hungarian Empire in 1918 (*see Map 38B*). The republic's initial problem was that Austria and its capital city of Vienna had been geared to the administration of a large empire, and then it suddenly found itself reduced to about one-tenth of its former size. Although the economic problems facing Austria were immense, the state was expressly forbidden by the Treaty of Saint Germain (1919) to seek union with Germany. Nevertheless, in March, 1938, Hitler accomplished the *Anschluss,* and Austria entered World War II as part of the German Reich.

After the war, from 1945 until 1955, Austria, like Germany, was divided into four zones and was occupied by the forces of three Western powers and the Soviet Union. Vienna was similarly divided and garrisoned. Unlike Germany, however, Austria was permitted to establish a national government as soon as the war ended. This fact prevented the division into zones from becoming dismemberment, as in Germany. As Austria had never declared war herself, a formal treaty of peace was not considered necessary. After prolonged negotiations with the Russians, an agreement was finally reached in 1955 that provided for the withdrawal of both the Allied and the Soviet forces in return for Austria's maintenance of a policy of neutrality similar to the one pursued by Switzerland. Austria's actions are today watched very closely by the Soviet Union to ensure that they do not stray from the narrow path of neutrality. This did not, however, prevent the Austrian Government from actively assisting the thousands of refugees who flooded into the country after the suppression of the Hungarian revolution in 1956, or from voting against the Communist bloc on numerous occasions in the United Nations.

As in the case of Switzerland, the politics of Austria rarely makes headlines, because it is concerned almost exclusively with internal affairs. The largest political parties are the Social Democratic, moderately socialist in tone, and the Catholic People's Party. All but the earliest postwar governments have been made up of a coalition of these two parties. The relative strengths of the two parties in the cabinet have been altered from time to time to reflect shifts in their electoral support. The President of the Republic is a Socialist, Adolf Scharf; the Chancellor, a chief executive, is the People's Party leader Alfons Gorbach. A third party, the Freedom Party, has enough seats

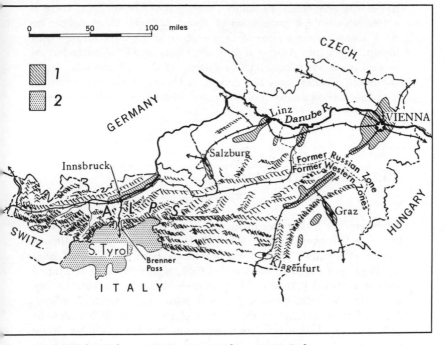

1—main industrial area; *2*—German-speaking area in Italy

in Parliament to represent a balance of power between the two major groups in case of a conflict between them. But since it is widely regarded as Nazi-tainted, the major parties are hesitant to seek its support.

Austria has now overcome the problem presented by the dismemberment of its former empire. Manufacturing industry, partly dependent on hydroelectric power, has been greatly expanded. Industry and banking are in large part government-owned. The area of agricultural land remains small (about 22 per cent of the total) and Austria depends heavily on imported foodstuffs, which she has to pay for by the export of manufactured goods and services. Forest products are an important export. Also, Austria is fast developing a large tourist trade.

A few small Slovene and Croat communities have remained within the boundaries of Austria, and they have occasionally been the basis of vague claims and assertions by Yugoslavia. In the province of Carinthia, in the southeastern part of the state, a plebiscite was held in 1920, but the vote in favor of union with Yugoslavia was very small. In South Tyrol, a province of Italy, there is a German-speaking population of about 222,000; these people regard Austria as the source of their culture and would perhaps seek incorporation into Austria if this were practicable. Austria has on several occasions taken steps to safeguard the cultural interests of the South Tyrolese and has served as the headquarters for South Tyrolese propagandists and terrorists, but officially she has never advocated the cession of this area to her.

49. The Little States

There are five little states in Europe, each of which has an area of less than 200 square miles. (One of them actually has less than a quarter of a square mile.) Four are survivals of small feudal principalities, and the fifth, the Vatican City, is a re-creation of a small state that ceased to exist in 1870. In each of them—the Vatican City excepted—the politics resembles local rather than national politics. None of them belongs to the United Nations, and each maintains only a minimal diplomatic representation in other countries. None has military forces of any significance, and in some—Monaco and Vatican City, for example—the small troop of soldiers are dressed and equipped in an antique fashion and provide spectacle rather than security. It might be argued that these diminutive states have been able to survive in an age of power politics only because the advantages to be gained by absorbing them have been outweighed by the disadvantage of incurring the ill will of other countries.

Andorra

Andorra is a small principality in the Pyrenees on the border between France and Spain. Sovereignty is jointly exercised by the Spanish Bishop of Urgel and the President of the French Republic, assisted by an elected General Council—an arrangement that has lasted effectively for nearly 700 years. Andorra has a population of only about 9,000. The language is Catalan. The principal economic activities are sheep-raising and smuggling.

Liechtenstein

Liechtenstein is situated between Switzerland and Austria and is in a customs union with Switzerland. It was created in the four-

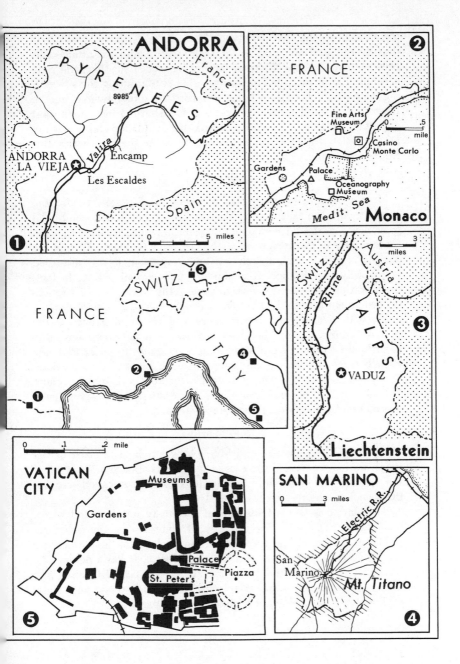

teenth century as the County of Vaduz. Its territory was subsequently rounded out, and in the eighteenth century it attained its present area. Perhaps the most interesting fact about this little state is simply that it managed to survive as an entity during the succeeding centuries, rather than being absorbed by either Switzerland or Austria. A limited monarchy under a Hapsburg prince, it is most important today as a haven for income-tax avoidance and a place of incorporation for companies wishing to keep their activities free from surveillance.

Monaco

Monaco, the most advertised of these small states, is also the smallest, with the exception of Vatican City. It originated as a feudal principality in the thirteenth century and has since remained almost continuously in the possession of the House of Grimaldi. During the periods of the French Revolution and Napoleon, it was absorbed temporarily into France. It is almost wholly urban and is, in fact, the most densely settled sovereign state in the world. Its chief source of income is the gambling casino of Monte Carlo. It is in a customs union with France, and the territory will revert to France if the present ruling family becomes extinct. France complains that Frenchmen habitually use Monaco as a residence in order to evade French taxes. Under the threat of a French blockade, Monaco recently reached an agreement with France that will make it more difficult for French individuals and corporations to escape French jurisdiction by acquiring a domicile in Monaco.

San Marino

Andorra, Liechtenstein, and Monaco lie either on a coast or between the boundaries of their larger neighbors. But San Marino and the Vatican City—the Holy See, as it is sometimes called—are entirely enclosed by the territory of Italy.

San Marino is the last survivor of the many separate and sovereign states that once made up Italy. It claims to be the oldest republic in the world and traces its origin back to the fourth century A.D.—a claim that few historians will agree with. It has a democratic form of government, and for a time its elected Grand Council had a Communist majority. San Marino is in a customs union with Italy, with which it has a treaty of friendship and alliance.

Vatican City

From early in the Middle Ages until 1870, the Popes of Rome exercised a temporal rule over a group of territories commonly known as the Papal States. The area of these states varied throughout their history, but at one time their territory formed an almost solid block reaching across the Italian peninsula. In 1860, most of the Papal States were absorbed into the kingdom of Italy. However, the Pope continued to hold Rome until 1870. From 1870 to 1929, the Pope had no temporal powers, but the Concordat of February, 1929, negotiated with the Italian Government, restored to the Papacy complete sovereignty over the city of the Vatican. Vatican City, with an area of 108.7 acres, thus became the smallest sovereign state in the world. The Italian Government also granted the Pope extraterritorial rights in certain of the churches of Rome, in his summer villa in the Alban Hills at Castel Gandolfo, and in the area occupied by the Vatican radio station at Santa Maria di Galeria. The Vatican City is politically neutral and continues its political relations even with countries with which Italy may be at war.

A large part of the Vatican City is taken up by the Vatican itself, the basilica of St. Peter's, and the piazza in front of it. There is normally a free right of entry and movement through the piazza, which is subject to the jurisdiction of the Italian police.

A. *Moorish invasion and reconquest:*
1—Moslem Empire, 750 A.D.; *2*—reconquest by the Christian states
B. *Major languages*
C. *Provinces and major industrial areas*

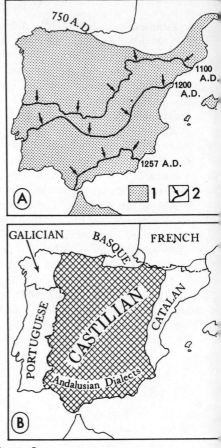

50. The Iberian Peninsula

The Iberian Peninsula, consisting of Spain and Portugal, enclosed on about seven-eighths of its circumference by the sea and on the remainder by the Pyrenees, looks as if it is the most distinctive of all the geographical divisions of Europe. Yet it has known political unity for a total of only about sixty years—during the late sixteenth and early seventeenth centuries. The peninsula has always been marked by its cultural and linguistic diversity.

Most of the peninsula consists of a plateau, the Meseta. Across it lie mountain ridges, and mountains enclose it on the north and south. The small areas of coastal lowland that fringe the peninsula,

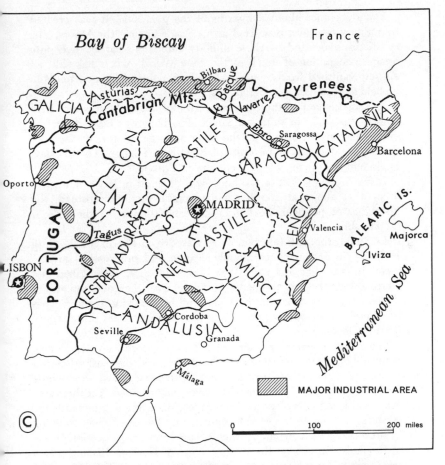

especially on the west and east, are somewhat cut off physically
both from the Meseta and from one another. Thus physical obstacles
alone have made political unity difficult to achieve.

In the eighth century, the region was overrun by the Moors—
Moslem invaders from North Africa. They never completely conquered the mountainous north, and a number of petty kingdoms
survived in the Pyrenees and the Cantabrian Mountains. As Moorish power grew weaker, these small states expanded southward, and
the last Moorish stronghold fell in 1492. The petty kingdoms
merged gradually with one another until, when Ferdinand of Aragon married Isabella of Castile, their number was reduced to two—
Portugal and Spain.

Spain occupies about five-sixths of the peninsula. It was created by military conquest disguised as a crusade against the Moors. The fanaticism generated by these military campaigns carried over into Spain's occupation of much of the New World, and it has still not entirely vanished from Spain itself, where political opinion tends to be held as zealously as religious opinion.

A second legacy of the conquest of the Moors is the mode of land tenure, especially in southern Spain. The land was taken from the infidel and given, mainly in the form of large estates, to the conquering aristocracy to be cultivated with serf labor. To this day, Spain remains the most feudal country in Europe.

In Portugal, the last of the kings was deposed in 1910 by a revolution that aimed at creating a democratic republic. Instead, the instability of political life led to the establishment of the Salazar dictatorship.

In Spain, the last Bourbon king was driven out in 1931. Until 1936, Spain had a democratically elected and progressive government. In that year, the Civil War broke out, and, with Italian and German help, Franco succeeded in taking over the government and the country. Franco is still in power, and his fascist government has completely reversed the progressive trend of legislation of its republican predecessor.

Spain and Portugal are among the most poorly developed economically, the most educationally backward, and the least advanced politically of the countries of Europe. Neither has known democratic forms of government for more than a very short period. Yet their geographical location is of great significance, since Spain commands the western entrance to the Mediterranean Sea. Portugal's long-standing alliance with Great Britain springs in part from her possession of one of the finest harbors on the western coast of Europe—Lisbon, which has facilities for refitting and providing refuge for British ships. The strategic significance of this region was more recently emphasized by the United States when it set up air bases in Spain after World War II.

The Iberian Peninsula is also better endowed by nature than other parts of Southern Europe. It has important reserves of coal and iron, as well as of many nonferrous ores, including copper, lead, zinc, tungsten, and mercury. Iron smelting has been developed in the Basque region of northern Spain.

The most advanced part of Spain is Catalonia, where the textile and other industries are well developed. This region has been almost traditionally opposed to the conservative and backward Meseta.

110

The language map of the Iberian Peninsula points up its cultural diversity. The dominant language is Castilian Spanish, which is spoken over the whole of the Meseta. Along the western margin, there are Galician dialects, closely related to Spanish, from one of which Portuguese developed. Along the Mediterranean coast, Catalan is spoken; in the south, the dialects of Andalusia; in the mountains of the north, the Basque language.

From each of these has sprung some kind of nationalist or separatist movement. Most distinct and successful has been Portugal, which, thanks largely to the support of British sea powers, has been independent for most of its history. The Catalan nation has been less fortunate. It formed the major part of the old Kingdom of Aragon, prior to its merger with Castile under Ferdinand and Isabella. But thereafter, despite several revolts against Spanish control, Catalonia was really autonomous only during the short-lived Spanish Republic (1931–39). The Basque territory, which in the Middle Ages constituted the Kingdom of Navarre and is distinctive in many ways from the rest of Spain, was autonomous for about the same period.

Both before and after this interlude, the Spanish Government has been centralized in Madrid, near the geometrical center of Spain. It was located there deliberately in the sixteenth century, in the hope that this would impose unity on the whole country.

Both Spain and Portugal retain extensive empires. Spain's empire, consisting of territories on the west coast of Africa, is thinly populated and unimportant. The Portuguese empire, however, includes the large and important African territories of Angola, Mozambique, and Portuguese Guiana, as well as the strategically important Azores and Cape Verde islands in the Atlantic, Macao (a small island off the China coast and an important center for the purchase by Communist China of articles embargoed by the U.S. and its allies), and part of the East Indian island of Timor.

51.   Gibraltar and Malta

Close to the southern tip of the Spanish peninsula is the Rock of Gibraltar, a mass of limestone that rises abruptly from the sea and is joined to the mainland only by a bank of sand and shingle. Its name is Moorish, and it was a landing place of the Moslem invaders about the year 710. In 1704, it was occupied by the British, who have held it ever since.

It lies just within the Strait of Gibraltar—at this point about 10 miles wide—and its guns are able to command the whole waterway. Gibraltar has been transformed into a military and naval base, but, as such, it presents certain problems: It does not have a good airfield, and one could not be constructed there except by the incorporation of land from Spain; it does not have an adequate water supply, since there is little rainfall on the rocks; it is largely dependent on Spanish workers who commute each day between Gibraltar and Spain; and, last, the Franco government claims from time to time that Gibraltar should be restored to Spain. Suggestions that it might be traded for a base—Ceuta, perhaps—on the opposite shore of the Strait, have never materialized.

The strategic importance of Gibraltar has been very much reduced by long-range aircraft. Its naval importance continues to be considerable, and it is a free port.

Malta consists of two islands, Malta and Gozo, lying between Sicily and Libya near the narrowest point of the Mediterranean Sea. They had long been held by the Knights of Malta against the Turks, but were occupied by the British in 1800, with the acquiescence of the Maltese, and they have since been part of the British Empire and Commonwealth. The port of Valletta, on the island of Malta, has been equipped as a naval station and is the chief base of the British Mediterranean fleet.

Malta is self-governing, although its foreign affairs are controlled by the British. The dockyards employ most of Malta's labor force, and contraction of British operations there has threatened the welfare of the islands. The people speak the distinctive Maltese language, which is basically a Semitic language derived from ancient Phoenician. A majority of the Maltese people formerly favored complete incorporation of the island into the United Kingdom, politically and economically. When Great Britain rejected this, they turned to a demand for independence, although realizing that it would conflict with their own economic interests.

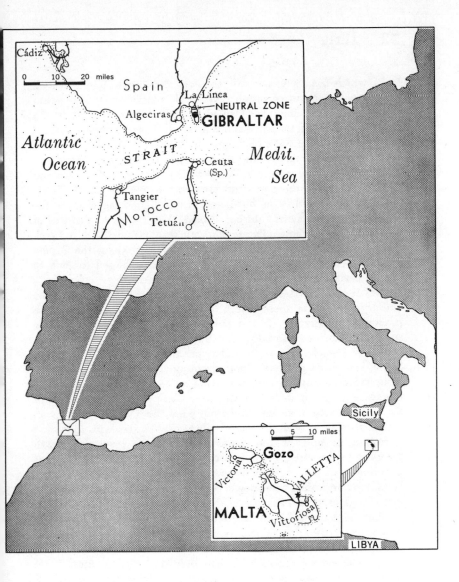

52. Italy

Italy, which has fewer natural resources than Spain and Portugal, has proved to be more progressive, both economically and politically. The modern Italy was formed in 1860, when, as a result of a popular movement, the small states of which it was composed joined together under the King of Savoy. In 1946, by popular vote, the monarchy was terminated and the Republic of Italy established.

As a result of her victory in World War I, Italy was able to extend her boundaries in the north and northeast to include South Tyrol, Venezia Giulia, and Istria, but failed to make good her claim to the Dalmatian coast. Defeat during World War II led to the loss of Istria and part of the Giulian region, but Italy retained South Tyrol, largely because her so-called natural boundary along the Alpine mountain crest included it. In 1947, Italy was obliged to cede to France certain very small territories in the French Alps.

Italy is characterized by strong local feeling in many parts of the country. In two of these—South Tyrol and the Aosta Valley—the predominant language is not even Italian. Most South Tyrolese speak German (*see Map 48*), and the inhabitants of the Aosta Valley speak French. The Aosta Valley and the islands of Sardinia and Sicily, have been granted a limited autonomy. The Tyrolese sought a similar autonomy; instead, they were made part of a larger autonomous region with an Italian majority. The present disturbances in South Tyrol arise from this, and from what the Tyrolese claim is an Italian attempt to swamp them by colonizing the area with Italians.

Italy is an industrialized country. Most of the industrial growth has been in the north, where hydroelectric power from the Alps has in recent years become very important, but for centuries the south—Il Mezzogiorno—has been neglected. This is now being corrected, and a huge program of land reclamation and industrial development is being implemented with resources from northern Italy. The south remains very overcrowded and by far the poorest part of the country. Emigration, both to northern Italy and to other countries, has long taken place on a large scale. Italian industry relies on imports for most of the raw materials it uses—fuel, ores, and fibers.

In the last years of the nineteenth century, Italy began to develop a colonial empire. This was lost during World War II, although Italy did retain Somalia until 1960 as a trusteeship territory.

In October, 1922, Mussolini, with his so-called March on Rome, overthrew the constitutional government and became the dictator—

1—main industrial area; *2*—highlands

Il Duce—of Fascist Italy. He carried through some minor internal reforms, invaded and conquered Ethiopia, intervened in the Spanish Civil War on the side of Franco, and took his country into World War II on the side of Germany. In July, 1943, he was removed from power and killed by Italian anti-Fascists as he tried to escape from Italy.

The democratic constitution was restored. In 1946, by a referendum, the Italian people decided to terminate the monarchy, and Italy became a republic. Since then there have been frequent changes of government, and because one party has seldom held a dependable majority, a coalition has usually been essential. At present, the Christian Democratic (Catholic) Party is much the largest, followed by the Communists and the Socialists. Italy has the largest Communist Party outside the Soviet bloc. Most governments since 1945 have been headed by Christian Democrats.

115

53. Greece

An independent and unified Greece never existed in classical times. The modern Greek state that came into existence in the nineteenth century considers itself the successor to the Byzantine Empire, a fact that has sometimes been reflected in its territorial claims. The Kingdom of Greece was established in 1830. The territory of Greece was subsequently extended by degrees until it embraced three sides of the Aegean Sea and a few islands along the fourth, or eastern, side. In 1947, the Dodecanese Islands, occupied since 1912 by the Italians, were ceded to Greece.

At the end of World War I, there was a substantial Turkish minority in Greece and a very much larger Greek minority in Turkey. The two countries agreed in 1923 to exchange their minorities. In the years following, the Greeks from Turkey were settled for the most part in the plains of Macedonia. Although a large part of the Albanian population and many Slavophobes were driven out of Greece in the postwar period, there are still some Albanians, while Slavophobe Bulgars and Macedonians form the majority of the population in some parts of Thrace and Macedonia. Other Thracian areas are predominantly Turkish, and there are small Italian minorities in the Dodecanese and Corfu. All Greece's neighbors except Italy periodically protest Greece's treatment of the minorities with which they have ethnic ties. Nevertheless, relations between Greece and Yugoslavia have in recent years been generally good. The most convenient access to the sea from the interior of Yugoslavia is across Greek Macedonia, and the Yugoslavs have long enjoyed a free zone in the port of Salonika.

Greece is a poor and mainly agricultural country. Its chief exports are tobacco, dried grapes in various forms, wine, olives, and a small quantity of minerals, of which the most important is bauxite. Its imports are manufactured goods and those foodstuffs that Greece finds it too expensive to grow because of the dry climate and the rugged terrain. Greece has a very large volume of trade in proportion to its population, and the merchant fleet, owned largely by expatriate Greeks and manned to a considerable extent by Greek seamen, is one of the largest in the world. But most of it is still registered under foreign flags, and its contribution to the Greek economy is relatively small. Tourism and emigrant remittances are two of Greece's most important economic resources.

Greece formerly had ambitious claims to territory on the mainland

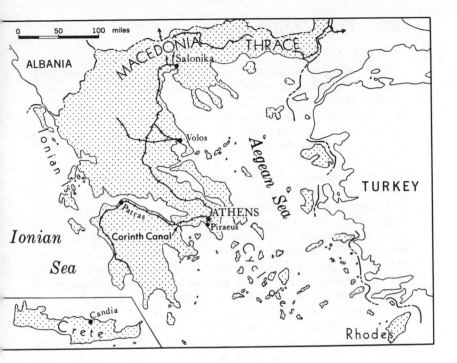

of Asia Minor, but her attempts to enforce them at the end of World War I failed disastrously. Since then, Greek relations with Turkey have improved; they were, however, seriously impaired by a dispute regarding the future of the formerly British-held island of Cyprus in the eastern Mediterranean.

Both Greece and Turkey feel themselves threatened either by the Soviet Union or by the satellite states of the Balkans. Greek relations with Yugoslavia, however, have greatly improved. Greece, like Turkey, has been the recipient of extensive United States aid, designed both to keep the country from Communism and, more important, to restore its economy. In both respects, the aid has proved successful so far, although the Greek Communist movement is still very strong and large-scale unemployment persists.

Greece is today a constitutional monarchy. The chief of state is King Paul I. The right-wing National Radical Union of Constantine Karamanlis has for the last several years had a parliamentary majority, which the opposition parties claim was secured by electoral fraud and intimidation.

54. The Mediterranean

To the ancients, the Mediterranean was the sea that lay in the middle of the world, as its name implies. The Roman Empire grew up around its shores, and the Roman provinces were held together by the Mediterranean sea routes that joined them. This unity, which turned the Mediterranean into a Roman lake, was ended during the Middle Ages when the Italian city states of Venice and Genoa challenged the Byzantine Empire on the sea, and the Arabs and, later, the Turks conquered first the southern and then the eastern shores. The sea then became a frontier, separating the cultural world of Europe from that of Africa and the Middle East, and it has remained substantially this ever since. European powers attempted, during the nineteenth and early twentieth centuries, to establish their control over the opposite, or southern, shore—the French occupying Morocco, Algeria, and Tunisia; the Italians Libya; the British Egypt; and the British and French, for a period of a few years, dividing the major part of the Arab Middle East between them. Under Mussolini, the Italians talked of following the Roman example by turning the sea into an "Italian lake," a project that failed completely.

The role of the Mediterranean was greatly changed by the opening of the Suez Canal in 1869. Previously, a small volume of commerce had gone overland from the Mediterranean, across the Middle East, to the Orient. Now a growing proportion of a rapidly expanding world trade used the Canal, and the freedom to continue to use it became essential to the nations of Western Europe. Possession of strategic bases such as Gibraltar, Malta, and Cyprus became increasingly important to Great Britain, which was the most important maritime and commercial state at that time. The threat to her commerce posed by Russia (and later by the Soviet Union) was serious, and Great Britain consolidated her control of the Suez Canal by occupying Egypt in 1882. Britain's later retention of Cyprus and her acceptance of the Palestinian mandate were understandable in light of the proximity of these areas to the vital Mediterranean-Suez routeway. Great Britain still has an air base on the territory of the independent and sovereign state of Cyprus; France retains naval bases in Algeria and Tunisia. The United States and Britain now have bases in Libya, as Italy formerly did. There are also NATO bases in Greece and Turkey, while the Soviet Union maintained a base in Albania until its rupture with that country.

Today, the route by which much of Europe's supply of petroleum

A. *Present Mediterranean area*
B. *The Roman Empire at the time of Trajan, 116* A.D.

reaches its destination is through the Suez Canal and the Mediterranean Sea. The economic and strategic importance of this route has, however, declined for the nations of Western Europe because of the discovery of alternative sources of petroleum in North Africa and the development of giant tankers capable of transporting oil economically around the Cape of Good Hope.

119

55. The European Community

Traditionally, the countries of Central and Western Europe have never been noted for their friendship and cooperation. This has changed, and in the last fifteen years a true European Community has begun to emerge. It is characterized by political and economic cooperation, and war between any of its members has become so inconceivable that, in the building of an industrial plant of vital importance, for example, they have to some extent been prepared to subordinate their national interests to the welfare of the group as a whole.

The chief architect of this Community was, in a sense, Joseph Stalin. Without the external threat from the Soviet Union and the internal danger of Communist subversion, it probably would not have been achieved. The actual architect was General George C. Marshall, the American Secretary of State, who, in 1947, offered economic assistance to European countries for the rebuilding of their economies, on the condition that they collaborate to divide American aid among them and to use it effectively.

By 1947, relations between the Western powers and the Soviet Union has deteriorated to the point where the former felt it necessary to take steps toward collective defense. The chief dates in the several movements that combined to create the European Community were:

1947—The Cold War became a reality. President Truman gave aid to Greece and Turkey, which were threatened by Communist revolution. On June 5, General Marshall proposed the Marshall Plan of aid to European countries. This led to the formation of the Organization for European Economic Cooperation (OEEC), replaced in 1961 by the Organization for Economic Cooperation and Development (OECD).

1948—The Brussels Treaty "for collaboration in economic, social, and cultural matters and for collective self-defense" was signed by the United Kingdom, France, and the Benelux countries, and was subsequently joined by Italy and the German Federal Republic. The Berlin blockade by the Russians and East Germans brought about the Allied airlift to provide supplies to Berlin.

1949—The Council of Europe was formed "to achieve a greater unity among its members for the purpose of safeguarding and realizing the ideals and principles which are their common heritage and of facilitating their economic and social progress." The North Atlantic Treaty Organization (NATO) was formed.

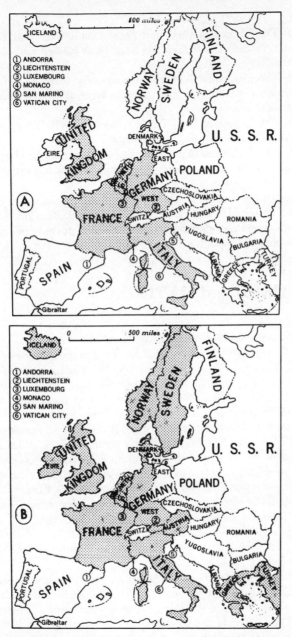

A. *Member countries of the Brussels group*
B. *Member countries of the Council of Europe*

1950—The European Coal and Steel Community was proposed by Robert Schuman of France. Its treaty was ratified and came into force in 1952.

1958—The European Economic Community (EEC), or Common Market, came into being. The Atomic Energy Community (Euratom) took shape.

1959—The European Free Trade Association (EFTA), otherwise known as the "Outer Seven," was formed.

1961 (July)—United Kingdom applied for membership in the European Economic Community; membership vetoed by France in 1963.

1961 (September)—OEEC, claiming that its tasks in Europe had been accomplished, turned itself into the Organization for Economic Cooperation and Development (OECD) for the purpose of emphasizing European aid to underdeveloped areas.

56.   OECD and NATO

The Organization for European Economic Cooperation, known as OEEC, was established in 1948 by the European beneficiaries of Marshall Plan aid. They were joined by the newly constituted German Federal Republic in 1949, and by Spain in 1959. Canada and the United States were closely associated with the OEEC from its inception. Its purpose was to develop economic cooperation between its members and to assist in carrying out the United States program of aid to Europe. The Marshall Plan terminated in 1952, but the collaboration of European states in the OEEC had been so fruitful that its members decided to make the organization permanent. In 1961, its name was changed to the Organization for Economic Cooperation and Development (OECD), a change that reflected the fact that its interests were no longer confined to Europe but now extended to all underdeveloped areas of the world. The United States and Canada, which had only been associated with the OEEC, were full members of the OECD.

The North Atlantic Treaty Organization was created a year after the OEEC. It grew out of the determination, expressed in the Brussels Treaty of 1948, of the West European nations to defend themselves. The United States took part in this military pact and almost at once became its most powerful member. The members of NATO pledged themselves to settle by peaceful means any disputes that

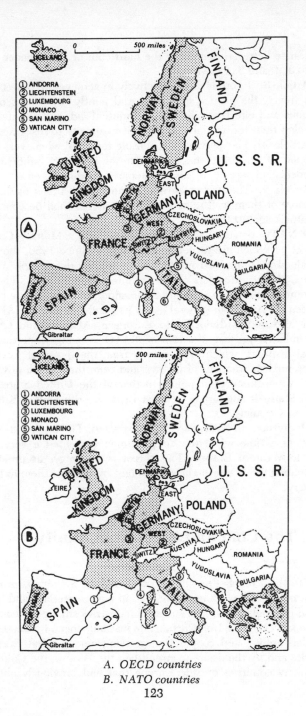

① ANDORRA
② LIECHTENSTEIN
③ LUXEMBOURG
④ MONACO
⑤ SAN MARINO
⑥ VATICAN CITY

A. OECD countries
B. NATO countries
123

might arise between them, but the hard core of the Alliance lay in articles 3, 4, and 5 of the treaty:

Article 3: In order more effectively to achieve the objectives of this treaty, the parties separately and jointly, by means of continuous and effective self-help and mutual aid, will maintain and develop their individual and collective capacity to resist attack.

Article 4: The parties will consult together whenever, in the opinion of any of them, the territorial integrity, political independence, or security of any of the parties is threatened.

Article 5: The parties agree that an armed attack against one or more of them in Europe or North America shall be considered an attack against them all.

The NATO powers have a Council and also a Military Committee, both of which are in permanent session. Since 1950, they have maintained an integrated military force for the defense of Western Europe. The headquarters of the organization is in Paris. The military command, under a supreme commander (who up to the present has been an American general), has its headquarters (SHAPE) in France also and is divided into European, Atlantic, and Channel commands. At present, the role of NATO is being jeopardized by internal disputes, which arise mainly from the desire of France to develop nuclear weapons of its own and from the French unwillingness to subordinate their policy to that of the United States. The United States is supported on most issues by the United Kingdom and West Germany.

Such divisions in NATO are to be expected. The organization was created at a time when the Soviet Union presented a very grave threat to Western Europe. This threat is no longer as great, and unity among the Western allies is thought by some of them to be less necessary.

57. The Coal and Steel Community

In 1950, the French Foreign Minister, Robert Schuman, proposed the formation of a common market in raw materials and partly finished products of the iron and steel industries among the countries of Europe west of the Iron Curtain. He was influenced by the feelings of understanding and cooperation growing among West European countries and by the desire to strengthen the West in the Cold War. Also, many countries outside Europe that had previously obtained

their iron and steel goods from West European countries were now
equipping themselves to manufacture their own. Unless the cost of
production in Europe could be reduced, it was assumed, many overseas markets would be lost. It is doubtful whether this reasoning was
sound, however, because the world market for steel was actually expanding at a far faster rate than was supposed possible at the time.

Schuman's invitation to form a common market was accepted by
only five other countries—Belgium, Luxembourg, the Netherlands,
West Germany, and Italy. Great Britain was highly interested in the
proposal, but believed that her interests would not be served by
joining it. The treaty creating the European Coal and Steel Community came into effect in August, 1952. The lowering of tariffs and
the removal of obstacles to the freedom of trade between the six
countries proceeded gradually, and the process was not completed
for the steel market until 1958, although a free market had, in fact,
been achieved earlier for materials such as ore and scrap metal.

The Community had to face two main problems, among others. One was that the Belgian coal-mining industry was superannuated and relatively inefficient, which made competition with the more efficient German industry extremely difficult. The solution was to grant the Belgian mines a degree of protection and government assistance until the coal-mining industry could be adapted and equipped to meet the competition in return for a Belgian agreement gradually to shut down many of the mines.

The other problem was the high cost of steel production in some of the older metallurgical centers, especially in France. Obsolescent and noncompetitive plants were closed, and the rest were equipped to meet the challenge of the more efficient.

After over ten years, the European Coal and Steel Community has succeeded in streamlining a large part of its production; it has reduced the inevitable increase in costs and has made the West European industry more competitive. The High Authority of the Community has no authority to choose the location of new mines and factories, but it does make recommendations, and it has proved to be very effective in guiding the choice of sites considered best for the Community as a whole.

The Community was also provided with a legal court competent to hear and decide cases related to alleged discrimination by national governments and institutions in favor of particular branches of the industry. It was clearly intended that competition should be absolutely free and that the price of commodities should reflect the cost of materials, labor, and transportation. This intrusion on the sovereignty of member states has been accepted with a minimum of protest.

58. The European Economic Community

The success of the Coal and Steel Community encouraged the development of more extensive economic cooperation among the members. The Six (member countries of the Community) agreed in the Treaty of Rome in 1957: (1) to remove gradually *all* barriers to trade in *all* commodities between them, and (2) to adopt by stages a common customs barrier between themselves and the rest of the world. The treaty became effective on January 1, 1958, when the first steps were taken to reduce trading barriers among The Six and to equalize external barriers. It was at first expected that it would take from twelve to fifteen years to establish the Common Market;

but The Six have made faster progress than was originally supposed possible, and the Economic Community will probably be created ahead of schedule. This will be a free-trade area second only to the United States in gross national product and the production of consumer goods, although probably behind the Soviet Union in the production of capital goods. The following table compares the EEC and the United States in certain key respects.

	EEC 1961	U.S. 1961
Area (in thousand square miles)	457.7	3,615.2
Population (in millions)	170.6	183.7
GNP (in billions of dollars)	154.1	424.5
GNP per capita (in dollars)	903	2,311
Steel production (in millions of metric tons)	73.2	88.9
Total exports (in billions of dollars)	32.3	20.8

The Six showed themselves to be dedicated to the creation of a true economic community, and they were prepared to see this economic association ripen into a political association—a kind of federation, perhaps. A number of European states were sympathetic to the idea of a customs union, but were unwilling for a variety of reasons to go as far as The Six had gone at this time. These joined to form the European Free Trade Association, made up of the United Kingdom, Norway, Sweden, Denmark, Austria, Switzerland, and Portugal. The reasons that held this group away from the Economic Community were both economic and political.

Political reasons included the statutory neutrality of Switzerland and Austria. Sweden, also, was strongly inclined toward neutrality. The United Kingdom at the time believed that membership in the Community would conflict with its ties and obligations to the Commonwealth. All these countries were fearful of the political overtones that the Community seemed to have.

The economic reasons were that these countries either did not want to expose certain sectors of their economy to competition or desired to retain certain external economic ties. Most of them relied heavily on low-cost agricultural imports from overseas countries, and did not wish to substitute the high-cost products of French and German farmers. In England's case, this economic motive was reinforced by her close political ties with such foreign suppliers as the United States, Argentina, and the Commonwealth countries.

Such was the reasoning that brought the Outer Seven together to establish the Free Trade Association outside the European Economic Community. The Association limited its freedom of trade to nonagricultural products; it did not aim to have a common external tariff, and it did not stand in the way of trading arrangements that its members had already concluded outside the group, such as the United Kingdom's Commonwealth ties. Finally, it had no political aspirations. All in all, it was less firmly tied together than the European Economic Community.

But the Outer Seven proved to be not particularly effective. The group was dominated by Great Britain, and the volume of trade between the remaining members was far smaller than their trade with the countries of the Common Market. Consequently, in the summer of 1961, Great Britain applied for membership in the European Economic Community and was followed by Norway and Denmark. Discussions continued until early in 1963. It became clear that there were two sets of problems. The first concerned the relation to the Community of the United Kingdom's fellow members of

128

the Commonwealth. The second was the opposition of France to admitting the United Kingdom to the Community. By compromises and concessions, the former might have been overcome. The latter has proved insuperable. France fears that the admission of the United Kingdom would end her own period of dominance within the Community and, furthermore, that it would serve to align the EEC more closely with the policies of the U.S. Government.

Index *

Adenauer, Konrad, 28
Adriatic Sea, 1, 40, 42
Aegean Sea, 1, 43, 45
Africa, 5, 12, 23, 50
Agriculture, 5, 6, 8, 9, 15, 18, 19, 20, 23, 24, 36, 37, 39, 44, 53
Ahvenanmaa (Alaand) Islands, 20
Albania, 11, 12, 13, 32, 33, 40, 42, 46
Albanian language, 11, 35
Algeria, 23, 54
Alpine mountain system, 1, 2, 3, 4, 8, 23, 47, 52
Alsace-Lorraine, 23, 27. *See also* Lorraine
Amsterdam, 10, 24, 26, 29
Andalusia, 50
Andorra, 49
Angola, 50
Animal husbandry, 15
Ankara, 45
Antrim, County, 16
Antwerp, 10, 24, 25, 26, 29
Aosta Valley, 52
Apennine Mountains, 1
Aquitaine, 23
Arabic, 23
Aragon, 50
Arctic Corridor, 19
Arctic Ocean, 1, 19
Attila, 34
Attlee, Clement, 14
Austria, 3, 4, 12, 13, 25, 27, 41, 42, 48, 58; *Anschluss*, 48
Austro-Hungarian Empire, 13, 36, 37, 38, 48, 55

Balkan Peninsula, 1, 11, 12, 13, 18, 34, 40
Baltic Sea, 1, 4, 7, 19, 21, 22
Basel, 29, 47
Basque (language and people), 11, 50
Bavaria, 4
Belfast, 16

Belgium, 3, 5, 9, 10, 12, 13, 15, 24, 25, 27, 57
Benelux Union, 24, 55
Berlin, 27, 29, 30, 31, 32, 55; Airlift, 30, 55
Bessarabia, 33, 39, 41
Black Sea, 1, 4, 41, 45
Bolshevik Revolution, 21
Bonn, 28
Bornholm, 22
Bosnia, 12, 42
Bosporus, 45
Bratislava, 41
Bremen, 10, 28
British Isles, 1, 2, 6, 7, 14, 22. *See also* Eire, Great Britain, Ireland, Wales
Brittany, 23
Brussels, 25
Brussels Treaty, 55, 56
Budapest, 38
Bukovina, 33
Bulgaria, 3, 4, 12, 13, 34, 41, 42, 44
Bulgars, 44
Burgundy, 23
Byzantine Empire, 53

Canada, 56
Canals, 4, 25, 29, 29. *See also* Transportation systems
Cantabrian Mountains, 50
Carinthia, 48
Carpathian Mountains, 1, 39
Caspian Sea, 1
Castel Gandolfo, 49
Castilian language, 50
Catalan language, 50
Catalonia, 50
Catholic People's Party (Austrian), 48
Catholicism, 12, 16, 34, 42, 47
Caucasus Mountains, 1
Celtic languages, 14, 16
Central Europe, 2, 3, 11, 12, 13
Ceuta, 51

* The numbers refer to *map numbers* and accompanying text, *not* to pages.

130

Thrace, 12, 43, 55
Timber. *See* Forests and forest resources
Timor, 50
Tin, 5
Tito (Josip Broz), 33, 42
Tobacco cultivation, 53
Transportation systems and waterways, 4, 9, 10, 21, 26, 27, 28, 29, 41, 45
Transylvania, 39
Trieste, 40, 42, 43
Truck farming, 6, 15, 24
Truman, Harry S., 55
Tundra, 3
Tungsten, 50
Tunisia, 54
Turkey, 12, 13, 42, 44, 45, 53, 55
Turkish people, 35, 44
Turkish Straits, 45
Tyrol, South, 48, 52
Tyrone, 16

Ukraine and Ukrainian peoples, 8, 35, 36, 37, 39
Ulster, 16
United States, 15, 32, 53, 54, 55, 56, 57, 58; overseas bases of, 17, 50, 54, 56
Ural Mountains, 1
Uralic languages, 11
Urgel, Bishop of, 49

Vaduz, 49

Valletta, 51
Vardar River, 40, 43
Vatican City, 12, 49
Venezia Guilia, 52
Venice, 54
Versailles, Treaty of, 27
Vienna, 48
Viipuri (Viborg), 19
Vilna, 36
Vistula River, 4
Voivodina, 42

Wales, 5, 14
Walloons, 25
Warsaw, 36
Warsaw Pact, 33
Waterways. *See* Transportation systems
Weimar Republic, 27
White Sea, 1
Wilson, Harold, 14
Winter War of *1939–40,* 19, 20
World War I, 13, 18, 21, 25, 27, 28, 31, 42, 52, 53
World War II, 11, 18, 19, 21, 23, 27, 28, 33, 34, 36, 37, 38, 39, 45, 46, 48, 52, 53

Yugoslavia, 3, 4, 5, 10, 11, 12, 13, 33, 35, 40, 41, 42, 48, 53

Zhivkov, Todor, 44
Zuider Zee, 26